JDBC™
Pocket Reference

D0591564

JDBC™
Pocket Reference

Donald Bales

O'REILLY®

Beijing · Cambridge · Farnham · Köln · Paris · Sebastopol · Taipei · Tokyo

JDBC™ Pocket Reference

by Donald Bales

Copyright © 2003 O'Reilly & Associates, Inc. All rights reserved.
Printed in the United States of America.

Published by O'Reilly & Associates, Inc., 1005 Gravenstein Highway North, Sebastopol, CA 95472.

O'Reilly & Associates books may be purchased for educational, business, or sales promotional use. Online editions are also available for most titles (*safari.oreilly.com*). For more information, contact our corporate/institutional sales department: (800) 998-9938 or *corporate@oreilly.com*.

Editor:	Jonathan Gennick
Production Editor:	Jane Ellin
Cover Designer:	Emma Colby
Interior Designer:	David Futato

Printing History:

January 2003:	First Edition.

0-596-00457-5
[C]   [3/03]

Contents

JDBC
Pocket Reference

Introduction

The JDBC API allows your Java programs to interact with almost any tabular data source. Originally designed for relational databases, JDBC now offers features and drivers that allow it to even read from spreadsheets and text files.

JDBC consists of a set of Java interfaces and some classes that define the functionality to allow you to read and write data from and to a data source (database). The interfaces are, in turn, implemented by a particular vendor's JDBC driver classes. Figure 1 shows the JDBC classes and interfaces that make up the core API.

Acknowledgments

I would like to thank my editor Jonathan Gennick for his tireless efforts to improve the readability of the book (which was like trying to fit an elephant into an envelope) and my technical reviewer, Eric Burke, for his great attention to detail. I would also like to thank the following O'Reilly personnel, whose efforts turned this book into a visual work of art: Jane Ellin, Matt Hutchinson, and David Futato. Most of all, I'd like to thank my daughter Kristyn and, especially, wife Diane for supporting my efforts to write another useful book.

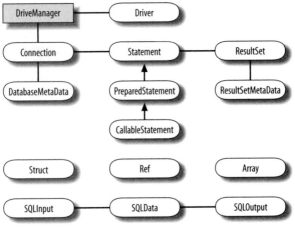

Figure 1. The interfaces of the core JDBC API

Conventions

Italic

Used for filenames, directory names, table names, field names, and URLs. It is also used for emphasis and for the first use of a technical term.

Constant width

Used for examples showing code, and for class and object names appearing in the text.

Constant width bold

Used to highlight important parts of code examples.

Constant width italic

Used to indicate variables within code examples.

[] Used in syntax descriptions to denote optional elements.

{} Used in syntax descriptions to denote a required choice.

| Used in syntax descriptions to separate choices.

... Used in syntax descriptions to indicate repeating elements. Also used in code examples to indicate code that was omitted because it isn't important to the example.

The Big Picture

To use JDBC, you start by establishing a database connection. To do so, load a driver and use `DriverManager`, or retrieve a `DataSource` via JNDI. Both return a `Connection` that will tell a `Statement` to execute a dynamic SQL Data Definition Language (DDL) or Data Manipulation Language (DML) statement, a `PreparedStatement` to execute a precompiled DML SQL statement, or a `CallableStatement` to execute a stored procedure. All three statement types return query results as a `ResultSet` that presents the data in a tabular form as a set of rows and columns. If a table, or any of the columns in a table, represents an SQL user-defined type (UDT) rather than an SQL built-in data type, you must update the `Connection`, `Statement`, `PreparedStatement`, or `CallableStatement`'s type map so JDBC knows which Java class to create for the corresponding UDT. The corresponding Java class itself must, in turn, implement the `SQLData` interface. See "User-Defined Data Types."

The primary resource for JDBC is Sun's web site at: *http:// java.sun.com/products/jdbc/*.

Import Statements

Table 1 is a list of possible imports to include in your program when using JDBC. At the very least, you'll need to import java.sql.*.

Table 1. JDBC-related imports

Import	Use
`java.sql.*;`	For Core JDBC support
`javax.sql.*;`	For Enterprise server-side support
`java.io.*;`	Support for streaming data types such as BLOB, CLOB, LONG, LONGRAW
`java.math.*;`	Provides `BigDecimal`, for numeric values

Table 1. JDBC-related imports (continued)

Import	Use
java.text.*;	Provides text formatting capabilities for dates and numbers
java.util.*;	Support for using properties

JDBC Drivers

JDBC drivers provide classes that implement the JDBC interfaces. Sun has a database with a search engine of available drivers at *htttp://industry.java.sun.com/products/jdbc/drivers*. Sun's search engine can tell you which drivers are available and where to obtain them.

Driver Types

JDBC defines four types of drivers. Each type employs a different architecture, each having a varying mix of operating system–dependent executable and Java code as follows:

Bridge (type 1)
> JDBC-ODBC bridge technology. A mix of Java and operating system–dependent code with which JDBC accesses a database through ODBC.

Native (type 2)
> Operating system–dependent executables and Java. A mix of Java and operating system–dependent code with which JDBC accesses a database through proprietary vendor code.

Network (type 3)
> Network middleware and Java. A mix of Java and server based operating system–dependent code with which JDBC accesses the database through the middleware.

Thin (type 4)
> 100% Java. A pure Java driver that requires no operating system–dependent code, which makes the driver 100% portable.

Database URLs

The following is the general syntax for a JDBC database URL: jdbc:*subprotocol*:*subname*

jdbc

> Communications protocol, always jdbc.

subprotocol

> Driver name.

subname

> Driver-specific reference to a database. The subname element in this syntax can get quite complex, and its format depends on the driver you are using.

The following sections describe popular drivers, detailing each driver's archive, the driver class that needs to be loaded, and the database URL syntax for the driver. With the exception of the Sun JDBC-ODBC driver, I list only the Type 4 URL syntax for two reasons: one, because only Type 4 drivers are portable, and that's in keeping with the spirit of Java itself, and two, to conserve space. I may also note the JDBC API level. At the time this was written, it was usually JDBC 2.0. See "The JDBC API" for an explanation of Java and JDBC API versions. Query the driver's source URL or the Sun JDBC driver database for information on other types of drivers.

The following sections are very terse and consist only of lists, formatted as follows:

Database Name   Driver Name
Description

The list items have the following meanings:

Get it online at:	The source URL where you can find the driver online
Archive:	The archive file or files for the driver
Driver:	The driver's class name that you must load to use the driver

URL syntax:	The URL syntax to use for the *subname* portion of a URL for the driver in question
Supported properties:	The properties supported by the driver
Notes:	Other information that may be helpful as you use the driver

IBM DB2

HOBLink JDRDA

A JDBC 2.0 type 4 driver for IBM DB/2.

Archive:	*JHJDBC.JAR*	
Driver:	hob.sql.JHJDBCDriver	
Type 4 URL syntax:	jdbc:HOB:*database_name*	
Supported properties:	user	password
	ipaddress	Ipport
	dbname	Creator
	sqlid	Extname
	crypto	ssldb

MS SQL Server/Sybase

FreeTDS

A free JDBC 1.0 type 4 driver for SQL Server and Sybase.

Get it online at:	*http://www.freetds.org/software.html*	
Archive:	*freetds_jdbc.jar*	
Driver:	com.internetcds.jdbc.tds.Driver	
URL syntax:	jdbc:freetds:sqlserver://*servername*/ *database*	
	jdbc:freetds:sqlserver://*servername*:*port*/ *database*	
	jdbc:freetds:sybase://*servername*/*database*	
	jdbc:freetds:sybase://*servername*:*port*/ *database*	
Supported properties:	CHARSET	user
	password	PROGNAME
	TDS	
Notes:	Port defaults to 1433 for SQL Server and to 7100 for Sybase.	

MS SQL Server/Sybase

A free JDBC 2.0 type 4 driver for SQL Server and Sybase.

Get it online at:	*http://jtds.sourceforge.net/*
Archive:	*jtds.jar*
Driver:	com.internetcds.jdbc.tds.Driver
DataSource:	*com.internetcds.jdbcx.tds.TdsDataSource*
Type 4 URL syntax:	jdbc:freetds:*server_type*://*server*[:*port*][/ *database*][;*property*=*value*]

Notes:	*server_type*
	    sqlserver or sybase
	
	port
	    Default of 1433 for SQL Server and 4000 for Sybase
	
	database
	    Default is *master*

MS SQL Server 2000

Microsoft's JDBC 2.0 type 4 driver for SQL Server 2000.

Get it online at:	*http://msdn.microsoft.com/downloads/default. asp?URL=/downloads/sample.asp?url=/ MSDN-FILES/027/001/779/ msdncompositedoc.xml*
Archive:	*msbase.jar, msutil.jar, mssqlserver.jar*
Driver:	com.microsoft.jdbc.sqlserver.SQLServerDriver
Type 4 URL syntax:	jdbc:microsoft:sqlserver://*server_name*: *port*[;*property*=*value*]
Supported properties:	DatabaseName HostProcess NetAddress Password PortNumber ProgramName SelectMethod SendStringParameters AsUnicode ServerName User
Notes:	The default port is 1433.

mySQL

A JDBC 2.0 type 4 driver for mySQL.

Get it online at:	*http://www.mysql.com/downloads/api-jdbc. html*
Archive:	*mysql-connector-java-2.0.14-bin.jar*
Driver:	com.mysql.jdbc.Driver
DataSource:	*com.mysql.jdbc.jdbc2.optional. MysqlDataSource*
Type 4 URL syntax:	jdbc:mysql://[*hostname*][:*port*]/ [*dbname*][*?param1=value1*][*&param2=value2*]
Supported properties:	User password autoReconnect maxReconnects initialTimeout maxRows UseUnicode characterEncoding relaxAutocommit ultraDevHack capitalizeTypeNames profileSql
Notes:	A new driver, Version 3, is in beta and should be available in winter, 2002.

Oracle

Oracle's JDBC 2.0 type 2 and 4 drivers.

Get them online at:	*http://otn.oracle.com/software/tech/java/sqlj_ jdbc*

Archive:	Java 1.2–1.3
	    classes12.zip, nls_charset12.zip, ocrs12.zip
	Java 1.4
	    ojdbc1.4.zip, nls_charset12.zip, ocrs12.zip

Driver:	Oracle8*i*
	    oracle.jdbc.driver.OracleDriver
	
	Oracle9*i*
	    oracle.jdbc.OracleDriver

DataSource:	*oracle.jdbc.pool.OracleDataSource*
Type 4 URL syntax:	Java 1.2–1.3 jdbc:oracle:thin:[*user/password*]@*host*: *port*:sid

Java 1.4
```
jdbc:oracle:thin:[user/password]@//
host[:port]/service
```
Notes: The default port is 1521.

PostgresSQL (v7.1)

A JDBC 2.0 type 4 driver for PostgresSQL.

Get it online at:	*http://jdbc.postgresql.org/*
Archive:	*pgjdbc2.jar*
Driver:	`org.postgresql.Driver`

Type 4 URL syntax:	`jdbc:postgresql:`*database* `[?property=value][&property=value]`
	
	`jdbc:postgresql://`*host/database* `[?property=value][&property=value]`
	
	`jdbc:postgresql://`*host:port/database* `[?property=value][&property=value]`

Supported properties:

`user`	`password`
`PGHOST`	`PGPORT`
`charSet`	`compatible`

Notes: Host defaults to *localhost* (not 127.0.0.1) and port defaults to 5432 (configurable at build time).

Sun JDBC-ODBC Bridge

This type 1 driver is part of the standard API release.

Driver:	`sun.jdbc.odbc.JdbcOdbcDriver`
DataSource:	*sun.jdbc.odbc.ee.DataSource*
Type 1 URL syntax:	`jdbc:odbc:`*data-source-name*`[;`*attribute-name=attribute-value*`]`

Supported properties:

`charSet`	`user`
`password`	`databaseName`
`loginTimeout`	

A type 2 driver for Sybase.

Get it online at:	*http://www.sybase.com/detail/ 1,6904,1009796,00.html*
Archive:	Sybase Version 4.2 *jconnect42.zip*
	Sybase Version 4.5 *jconnect45.zip*
	Sybase Version 5.2 *jconnect52.zip*
	Sybase Version 5.5 *jconnect55.zip*
Driver:	4.x *com.sybase.jdbc.SybDriver*
	5.x *com.sybase.jdbc2.jdbc.SybDriver*
Type 4 URL syntax:	jdbc:sybase:Tds:*host*:*port*[,*property=value*]
	jdbc:sybase:jndi:[,*property=value*]
Supported properties:	Too many to list

NOTE

Make sure you know the driver's version number, which you can get from the documentation, because you must set it before connecting.

Establishing a Connection

A Connection represents a physical connection to a data source (database). Connections are used to create Statements, to prepare PreparedStatements, to prepare CallableStatements, and to manage transactions. You have two choices for establishing a connection. You can use the DriverManager facility, which is typical for unmanaged environments such as a standalone application, or you can use JNDI to retrieve a DataSource, which is typical for a managed environment such as an EJB running in an application server.

Using DriverManager

If you use the DriverManager facility to establish a connection, you need to know three things:

- The JDBC driver's class name
- The JDBC driver's database URL syntax
- The database's connection information

See "JDBC Drivers" for more information on how to determine a driver's class name and URL syntax.

Loading a JDBC driver

To load a JDBC driver, use the Class. forName(*driverClassName*) method as follows:

```
String driver = "sun.jdbc.odbc.JdbcOdbcDriver";
try {
  Class.forName(driver).newInstance( );
}
catch (Exception e) {
  e.printStackTrace( );
  System.exit(1);
}
```

Once the driver is loaded, you can choose one of the following three getConnection( ) methods to establish a connection:

Connecting with a URL, username, and password
    The first of the three methods requires you to pass a database URL, username, and password as follows:

```
Connection conn = null;
String password = "guest";
String     url = "jdbc:odbc:jdbcpr_mdb";
String     user = "anonymous";
try {
  conn = DriverManager.getConnection(
          url, user, password);
}
catch (SQLException e) {
  System.err.println(
```

```
          "Error connecting with " +
          "URL, user, & password");
        System.err.println(
          "errorCode=" + e.getErrorCode( ));
        System.err.println(
          "message=" + e.getMessage( ));
        System.exit(1);
    }
```

Connecting with a URL and properties

The second getConnection( ) method requires you to
pass a database URL along with a Properties object that
contains any other required or optional parameters
(which vary from driver to driver) such as user and
password. For example:

```
    Connection conn = null;
    String password = "guest";
    String     url = "jdbc:odbc:jdbcpr_mdb";
    String     user = "anonymous";
    try {
      Properties prop = new Properties( );
      prop.setProperty("user", user);
      prop.setProperty("password", password);
      conn = DriverManager.getConnection(url, prop);
    }
    catch (SQLException e) {
      ...
    }
```

Connecting with only a URL

The last getConnection( ) method requires only a database URL. Often, when using only a database URL,
properties are appended to the URL. Each vendor has its
own proprietary syntax for including properties such as
user and password as part of the database URL. Here's an
example using the JDBC-ODBC Bridge:

```
    String url = "jdbc:odbc:jdbcpr_mdb" +
                 ";user=guest" +
                 ";password=anonymous";
    try {
      conn = DriverManager.getConnection(url);
    }
    catch (SQLException e) {
      ...
    }
```

Using JNDI

A second option for establishing a connection is to invoke getConnection( ) on a DataSource object retrieved via JNDI. A DataSource or one of its siblings, a ConnectionPoolDataSource or an XADataSource, are all configured on a directory server by an administrator. Given the logical name for a data source configured on your host application server, you can use JNDI to retrieve a DataSource and then a Connection. The following example of this technique uses jdbcpr_mdb as the logical data source name:

```
Context    ctx  = null;
DataSource ds   = null;
Connection conn = null;
try {
  ctx  = new InitialContext( );
  ds   = (DataSource) ctx.lookup("jdbcpr_mdb");
  conn = ds.getConnection( );
}
catch (Exception e) {
  System.err.println(e.getMessage( ));
}
```

Examining DatabaseMetaData

You can use DatabaseMetaData to determine a database's capabilities at runtime. Call a connection's getMetaData( ) method to get a DatabaseMetaData object for the current connection as follows (assuming a Connection, conn, already exists):

```
DatabaseMetaData dbmd = null;
try {
  dbmd = conn.getMetaData( );
}
catch (SQLException e) {
  ...
}
```

See "DatabaseMetaData" in "The JDBC API" for detailed information on this topic.

Executing Dynamic SQL

You can use a Statement to dynamically execute SQL DDL or DML statements. You get a Statement from a Connection, conn, by calling its createStatement( ) method as follows:

```
Statement stmt = null;
try {
  stmt = conn.createStatement( );
  ...
}
catch (SQLException e) {
  ...
}
```

Statement has three methods you can use to execute SQL: execute( ), executeUpdate( ), and executeQuery( ). Which you use depends on the type of SQL statement you are executing.

Executing DDL

execute( ) is best suited for DDL or truly dynamic SQL. It returns true if an SQL statement's execution generates a result set, and you can then call Statement's getResultSet( ) method to get that result set. If execute( ) returns false, you can call Statement's getUpdateCount( ) to determine the number of rows affected by a DML statement. If there's an error generated by executing the DDL, an SQLException will be thrown. Here's an example in which I create a table named PERSON (assuming a Connection, conn, already exists):

```
Statement stmt = null;
try {
  stmt = conn.createStatement( );
  stmt.execute(
    "create table PERSON ( " +
    "person_id  integer  not null  primary key, " +
    "last_name  varchar(30), " +
    "first_name varchar(30), " +
    "birth_date date, " +
    "gender     varchar(1) ) ");
```

```
      stmt.close();
      stmt = null;
    }
    catch (SQLException e) {
      ...
    }
    finally {
      if (stmt != null)
        try { stmt.close(); } catch (Exception i) { }
    }
```

Executing INSERT, UPDATE, or DELETE Statements

executeUpdate() is well suited for executing DML statements other than SELECT, and returns the number of rows
affected by an SQL statement's execution. Here's an example in which I insert a row into the PERSON table created in
the previous section (assuming a Connection, conn, already
exists):

```
    int       rows = 0;
    Statement stmt = null;
    try {
      stmt = conn.createStatement();
      rows = stmt.executeUpdate(
        "insert into PERSON ( " +
        "        person_id, " +
        "        last_name, " +
        "        first_name, " +
        "        birth_date, " +
        "        gender ) " +
        "values ( " +
        "        1, " +
        "        'DOE', " +
        "        'JOHN', " +
        "        { d '1980-01-01' }, " +
        "        'M' ) ");
      stmt.close();
      stmt = null;
      if (rows != 1) {
        System.err.println(
          "Statement error: " +
          rows + " inserted. ");
```

```
    }
  }
  catch (SQLException e) {
    ...
  }
  finally {
    if (stmt != null)
      try { stmt.close( ); } catch (Exception i) { }
  }
```

Executing SELECT Statements

executeQuery( ) returns a ResultSet, which is well suited for executing an SQL SELECT statement. Here, I execute a query against the PERSON table (assuming a Connection, conn, already exists):

```
ResultSet rset = null;
Statement stmt = null;
try {
   rows = 0;
   stmt = conn.createStatement( );
   rset = stmt.executeQuery(
     "select person_id, " +
     "       last_name, " +
     "       first_name, " +
     "       birth_date, " +
     "       gender " +
     "from   PERSON " +
     "where  person_id = 1 ");
   while (rset.next( )) {
     rows++;
     personId  = rset.getInt(1);
     lastName  = rset.getString(2);
     firstName = rset.getString(3);
     birthDate = rset.getDate(4);
     gender    = rset.getString(5);
     System.out.println(
       personId  + "\t" +
       lastName  + "\t" +
       firstName + "\t" +
       birthDate + "\t" +
       gender );
   }
   rset.close( );
   rset = null;
```

```
      stmt.close();
      stmt = null;
    }
    catch (SQLException e) {
      ...
    }
    finally {
      if (rset != null)
        try { rset.close(); } catch (Exception i) { }
      if (stmt != null)
        try { stmt.close(); } catch (Exception i) { }
    }
```

You may have noticed in the last three examples that I always close the Statement. Closing a Statement as soon as it is no longer needed reduces resource consumption in both your program and in the database.

Executing Precompiled SQL

Using a PreparedStatement to execute SQL statements can be more efficient for your program and database, and easier to code. You get a PreparedStatement from a Connection, conn, by calling its preparedStatement( ) method as follows:

```
    PreparedStatement pstmt = null;
    try {
      pstmt = conn.prepareStatement(
        "insert into PERSON ( " +
        "        person_id, " +
        "        last_name, " +
        "        first_name, " +
        "        birth_date, " +
        "        gender ) " +
        "values ( " +
        "        ?, " +
        "        ?, " +
        "        ?, " +
        "        ?, " +
        "        ? ) ");
    }
    catch (SQLException e) {
      ...
    }
```

A PreparedStatement is most efficient if you can prepare it once but use it multiple times. It can be easier to code with because it frees you from having to write complex string concatenations and from using proprietary date-formatting methods to formulate an SQL statement. Instead, you use a question mark (?) as a placeholder for each input parameter and programmatically set the values for each placeholder before the SQL statement is executed.

Since PreparedStatement extends Statement it has all three execute methods just like Statement. It also has a set of mutator methods, or setXXX( ) methods, that are used to set the values for the placeholders (?) before execution, as shown in the following example. For this example, assume that a Connection, conn, and a PreparedStatement, pstmt, from the previous example, already exist.

```
try {
  pstmt.setInt(1, 2);
  pstmt.setString(2, "DOE");
  pstmt.setString(3, "JANE");
  pstmt.setDate(4,
    java.sql.Date.valueOf("1980-01-01"));
  pstmt.setString(5, "F");
  rows = pstmt.executeUpdate( );
  pstmt.close( );
  pstmt = null;
  if (rows != 1) {
    System.err.println(
      "Prepared statement error: " +
      rows + " inserted.");
  }
}
catch (SQLException e) {
  ...
}
```

The placeholders (?) are referenced by the mutator methods in the SQL statement starting with 1 and incrementing from left to right. So, in this example, the person_id in position 1 is set to an int value of 2. The last_name in position 2 is set to a String value of "DOE". After all the parameters are set, the statement is executed by a call to PreparedStatement's executeUpdate( ) method. Since an SQL statement is prepared, it is not passed as a parameter value to any of PreparedStatement's execute methods.

Executing a Stored Procedure

If deriving or storing a single unit of data for a program requires that many SQL statements be executed, it is more efficient to use a stored procedure than to execute all such SQL statements one at a time from a client. Use a CallableStatement to execute a stored procedure. You can get a CallableStatement from a Connection, conn, by calling its prepareCall( ) method as follows:

```
CallableStatement cstmt = null;
try {
  cstmt = conn.prepareCall(
    "{ ? = call add( ?, ? ) }");
  ...
}
catch (SQLException e) {
  ...
}
```

See "Escape Syntax" for details on the stored procedure call syntax. CallableStatement extends PreparedStatement, so, not surprisingly, it uses placeholders (?) for parameters—this time, however, for both IN, OUT, and IN/OUT parameters. After the stored procedure's call is prepared and before it is executed, you must do the following:

- Any OUT parameters must be registered using registerOutParameter( ), which takes two parameters. The first is the position of the placeholder (?) in the prepared call, starting with 1 and incrementing from left to right. The second is one of the java.sql.Types constants that tells the driver what kind of data is being returned from the stored procedure.

- Any IN and IN/OUT parameter values must be set using one of the setXXX() methods that is appropriate for the database's data type. For example:

```
try {
  cstmt = conn.prepareCall(
    "{ ? = call add( ?, ? ) }");
  cstmt.registerOutParameter(1, Types.NUMERIC);
  cstmt.setDouble(2, 1.0);
  cstmt.setDouble(3, 1.0);
  ...
}
catch (SQLException e) {
  ...
}
```

To execute a stored procedure, use the execute() method. To get any OUT parameter values from a stored procedure call, use one of CallableStatement's accessor or getXXX() methods that is appropriate for the SQL data type as shown in the following example:

```
double answer = 0.0;
try {
  cstmt = conn.prepareCall(
    "{ ? = call add( ?, ? ) }");
  cstmt.registerOutParameter(1, Types.NUMERIC);
  cstmt.setDouble(2, 1.0);
  cstmt.setDouble(3, 1.0);
  cstmt.execute();
  answer = cstmt.getDouble(1);
  cstmt.close();
}
catch (SQLException e) {
  ...
}
finally {
  if (cstmt != null)
    try { cstmt.close(); }
    catch (SQLException i) { }
}
```

Retrieving Query Results

The results of a SELECT statement are returned from executeQuery( ) as a ResultSet. A ResultSet mimics the result set of a query as a table with rows and columns. A ResultSet can be scrollable, updateable, and sensitive to database changes (if supported by the driver and database in question). By default, you can only scroll forward, one row at a time, through a result set; you cannot update any of the column values, nor can the driver detect database changes. To create a scrollable, updateable, or update-sensitive ResultSet, use one of Connection's alternate createStatement( ), prepareStatement( ), or prepareCall( ) methods. These methods take two additional arguments:

A ResultSet *concurrency constant*
> Specifies whether a result set will be read-only or updateable. Use one of the following two ResultSet constants:
>
>> CONCUR_READ_ONLY
>> CONCUR_UPDATABLE

A ResultSet *type constant*
> Specifies whether you can scroll in a result set created by the statement in question, and if the driver can detect changes to the result set in question in the database. Use one of the following ResultSet constants:

TYPE_FORWARD_ONLY
> For a forward-only, scrollable, update-insensitive result set

TYPE_SCROLL_INSENSITIVE
> For a bi-directionally scrollable, update-insensitive result set

TYPE_SCROLL_SENSITIVE
> For a bi-directionally scrollable, update-sensitive result set

Here's an example that creates a scrollable, updateable, sensitive ResultSet (assuming a Connection, conn, already exists):

```
ResultSet rset = null;
Statement stmt = null;
try {
  rows = 0;
  stmt = conn.createStatement(
    ResultSet.CONCUR_UPDATABLE,
    ResultSet.TYPE_SCROLL_SENSITIVE);
  rset = stmt.executeQuery(
    "select person_id, " +
    "       last_name, " +
    "       first_name, " +
    "       birth_date, " +
    "       gender " +
    "from   PERSON " +
    "where  person_id = 1 ");
  ...
}
catch (SQLException e) {
  ...
}
```

Navigating a Result Set

If a result set is forward-only scrollable, use the next( ) method to move forward through it one row at a time. This is typically done in a while loop as follows (assuming a Connection, conn, already exists):

```
ResultSet rset = null;
Statement stmt = null;
try {
  rows = 0;
  stmt = conn.createStatement( );
  rset = stmt.executeQuery("select ...");
  while (rset.next( )) {
    ...
  }
  ...
}
catch (SQLException e) {
  ...
}
```

If a result set is bi-directionally scrollable, you can use any of the following methods to position the cursor (row pointer): absolute( ), first( ), last( ), next( ), previous( ), or relative( ). For either kind of scrollability, you can use any of the following methods to determine the position of the cursor: isAfterLast( ), isBeforeFirst( ), isFirst( ), isLast( ), or getRow( ).

Accessing Column Values

Regardless of the type of ResultSet, to get the value for a column, use the getXXX( ) accessor method that is appropriate for that column's SQL data type. The accessor's first argument is the column index, which is the relative position of the column in the SQL statement, starting with 1 and incrementing from left to right. Here's an example (assuming a Connection, conn, already exists):

```
int          personId  = 0;
String       lastName   = null;
String       firstName  = null;
java.sql.Date birthDate = null;
String       gender     = null;
int          rows       = 0;
ResultSet    rset       = null;
Statement    stmt       = null;
try {
  stmt = conn.createStatement( );
  rset = stmt.executeQuery(
    "select person_id, " +
    "       last_name, " +
    "       first_name, " +
    "       birth_date, " +
    "       gender " +
    "from   PERSON " +
    "where  person_id = 1 ");
  while (rset.next( )) {
    rows++;
    personId  = rset.getInt(1);
    lastName  = rset.getString(2);
    firstName = rset.getString(3);
    birthDate = rset.getDate(4);
```

```
   gender      = rset.getString(5);
   ...
   }
   rset.close( );
   rset = null;
   stmt.close( );
   stmt = null;
}
catch (SQLException e) {
   ...
}
finally {
   if (rset != null)
      try { rset.close( ); } catch (Exception i) { }
   if (stmt != null)
      try { stmt.close( ); } catch (Exception i) { }
}
```

In this example, the int variable personId is set to the value of column person_id, which is in position 1, using the ResultSet accessor getInt( ) with a column index of 1. The String variable lastName is set to the value of column last_name using the accessor getString( ) with a column index of 2.

Inserting, Updating, and Deleting Rows in a ResultSet

If you have an updateable ResultSet, you can insert new rows, update the values of current rows, or delete rows.

Inserting a new row in an updateable ResultSet involves first moving to the *insert row* (a scratch pad area where you define a new row) with moveToInsertRow( ). Then, use the mutator, or updateXXX( ), methods to set the column values. Next, you actually insert the row with insertRow( ). Finally, move the cursor out of the insert row using moveToCurrentRow(), which will take you back to the row you were on before you started the insert process.

Updating an existing row in a ResultSet involves navigating to the desired row and then using the mutator, or updateXXX( ), methods to set the new column values. Last, you actually update the row with a call to updateRow( ).

Deleting an existing row in a ResultSet involves navigating to the desired row, then deleting the row with a call to deleteRow( ).

The following example shows all three operations (assuming a Connection, conn, already exists):

```java
ResultSet rset = null;
Statement stmt = null;
try {
  stmt = conn.createStatement(
    ResultSet.CONCUR_UPDATABLE,
    ResultSet.TYPE_SCROLL_SENSITIVE);
  rset = stmt.executeQuery(
    "select person_id, " +
    "       last_name, " +
    "       first_name, " +
    "       birth_date, " +
    "       gender " +
    "from   PERSON ");

  // Insert a row.
  rset.moveToInsertRow( );
  rset.updateInt(1, 3);
  rset.updateString(2, "DOUGH");
  rset.updateString(3, "PLAY");
  rset.updateNull(4);
  rset.updateNull(5);
  rset.insertRow( );
  rset.moveToCurrentRow( );

  // Update a row.
  rset.absolute(1);
  rset.updateString(2, "DOUGH");
  rset.updateRow( );

  // Delete a row.
  rset.absolute(1);
  rset.deleteRow( );

  rset.close( );
  rset = null;
```

```
    stmt.close( );
    stmt = null;
}
catch (SQLException e) {
    ...
}
finally {
    if (rset != null)
        try { rset.close( ); } catch (Exception i) { }
    if (stmt != null)
        try { stmt.close( ); } catch (Exception i) { }
}
```

Dynamically Determining Result Set Characteristics

You can use ResultSetMetaData to determine a ResultSet's characteristics at runtime. There are many reasons you might want to do this. For example, after issuing a dynamic SELECT statement, you would use ResultSetMetaData to determine just what that SELECT statement returned.

Call a result set's getMetaData( ) method to get a ResultSetMetaData object for the current result set as follows (assuming a Connection, conn, already exists):

```
int               cols = 0;
ResultSet         rset = null;
Statement         stmt = null;
ResultSetMetaData rsmd = null;
try {
    stmt = conn.createStatement( );
    rset = stmt.executeQuery(
        "select person_id, " +
        "       last_name, " +
        "       first_name, " +
        "       birth_date, " +
        "       gender " +
        "from   PERSON " +
        "where  person_id = 1 ");
    while (rset.next( )) {
        rows++;
        if (rows == 1) {
            rsmd = rset.getMetaData( );
```

```
            cols = rsmd.getColumnCount( );
            if (cols > 0) {
              for (int i = 1;i <= cols;i++) {
                if (i > 1) {
                  System.out.print("\t" +
                    rsmd.getColumnName(i));
                }
                else {
                  System.out.print(
                    rsmd.getColumnName(i));
                }
              }
              System.out.println("");
            }
          }
          if (cols > 0) {
            for (int i = 1;i <= cols;i++) {
              if (i > 1) {
                System.out.print("\t" +
                  rset.getString(i));
              }
              else {
                System.out.print(
                  rset.getString(i));
              }
            }
            System.out.println("");
          }
        }
        rset.close( );
        rset = null;
        stmt.close( );
        stmt = null;
      }
      catch (SQLException e) {
        ...
      }
```

Using the ResultSetMetaData object, the program first deter-
mines the number of columns in the SQL query. For the first
row in the result set, the program prints the column head-
ings using the column names from the database. Then it
prints the actual column values for each row. See "ResultSet-
MetaData" in "The JDBC API" for more information on all
of ResultSetMetaData's capabilities.

SQL/Java Data Type Mapping

Table 2 lists the *default* mapping between SQL and Java data types. Typically, you should use an accessor or mutator that gets or sets (or updates) the SQL data type with one of the listed Java data types, or vice versa.

Table 2. SQL and Java type mapping

SQL	Java
CHAR	java.lang.String
VARCHAR	java.lang.String
LONGVARCHAR	java.lang.String
NUMERIC	java.math.BigDecimal
DECIMAL	java.math.BigDecimal
BIT	boolean
BOOLEAN	boolean
TINYINT	byte
SMALLINT	short
INTEGER	int
BIGINT	long
REAL	float
FLOAT	double
DOUBLE	double
BINARY	byte[ ]
VARBINARY	byte[ ]
LONGVARBINARY	byte[ ]
DATE	java.sql.Date
TIME	java.sql.Time
TIMESTAMP	java.sql.Timestamp
CLOB	java.sql.Clob
BLOB	java.sql.Blob
ARRAY	java.sql.Array

Table 2. SQL and Java type mapping (continued)

SQL	Java
DISTINCT	Mapping of underlying type
STRUCT	java.sql.Struct
REF	java.sql.Ref
DATALINK	java.net.URL
JAVA_OBJECT	Underlying Java class

Handling NULL Values

Java does not have a corresponding concept for SQL NULL values. A Java null is not the same thing as an SQL NULL. When you use an accessor method to get a column value from a result set or stored procedure call, you have two ways of knowing whether the column value is NULL:

- You can call ResultSet's wasNull( ) method immediately after calling an accessor that returns a Java primitive type.

- Instead of using a primitive Java data type (like int), you can use an object type variable (like BigDecimal) along with an accessor that returns an object type (also like BigDecimal) as the recipient of the value from the accessor. Any SQL NULL values will then translate to null object references.

To set a column to an SQL NULL value, you must use one of the NULL mutators, setNull( ) or updateNull( ). Setting an object variable to null and passing it as a method's parameter will not work.

Detecting NULL Values with wasNull( )

The primitive Java data types such as int, long, and double cannot be null. Most are initialized to a value of 0. An accessor that returns a primitive—such as getInt( ), getLong( ), getDouble( ), etc.—returns a value of 0 when a database column is NULL. If you use wasNull( ) along with a primitive wrapper class such as Integer, Long, or Double, you can detect if the database column was NULL and set the wrapper class to a null pointer to keep track of the NULL values as follows (assuming a Connection, conn, already exists):

```
ResultSet rset = null;
Statement stmt = null;
Integer   numb = null;
try {
  stmt = conn.createStatement( );
  rset = stmt.executeQuery(
    "select to_number( NULL ) " +
    "from   DUAL ");
  while (rset.next( )) {
    numb = new Integer(rset.getInt(1));
    if (rset.wasNull( )) numb = null;
  }
  rset.close( );
  rset = null;
  stmt.close( );
  stmt = null;
}
catch (SQLException e) {
  ...
}
```

Detecting NULL Values with BigDecimal

Another alternative for detecting a column with NULL values is to use java.math.BigDecimal to hold numeric values in your program. BigDecimal is the only numeric object type that has a ResultSet accessor and mutator. As with all accessors that return object types, getBigDecimal( ) sets a BigDecimal variable to a null pointer if a database column has NULL values. Here's an example using BigDecimal (assuming a Connection, conn, already exists):

```
ResultSet  rset = null;
Statement  stmt = null;
BigDecimal bigd = null;
```

```
try {
  stmt = conn.createStatement( );
  rset = stmt.executeQuery(
    "select to_number( NULL ) " +
    "from   DUAL ");
  while (rset.next( )) {
    bigd = rset.getBigDecimal(1);
  }
  rset.close( );
  rset = null;
  stmt.close( );
  stmt = null;
}
catch (SQLException e) {
  ...
}
```

Setting a Column to a NULL Value

If you need to set a column to a NULL value, you can't sim-ply use null as the second argument (value) of a ResultSet, PreparedStatement, or CallableStatement mutator. Instead, you must use ResultSet's updateNull( ) or the setNull( ) method supported by both PreparedStatement and CallableStatement. updateNull( ) takes one argument, which is the column index. setNull( ) takes two arguments. The first is the column or parameter index; the second is one of the java.sql.Types constants, which specifies the SQL data type of the column or parameter that is to be set to NULL.

Batching Inserts and Updates

If you need to perform multiple iterations of the same SQL INSERT or UPDATE statement, then batching those state-ments will dramatically reduce the amount of time it takes for them to execute. Batching sends multiple SQL statements to the database simultaneously. When you batch statements, you call addBatch( ) instead of executeUpdate( ). At an inter-val specified by your code, you call executeBatch( ) to send a group of statements in one transmission. Here's an example (assuming a Connection, conn, already exists):

```
PreparedStatement pstmt = null;
try {
  conn.setAutoCommit(false);
  pstmt = conn.prepareStatement(
    "insert into PERSON ( " +
    "          person_id, " +
    "          last_name, " +
    "          first_name, " +
    "          birth_date, " +
    "          gender ) " +
    "values ( " +
    "          ?, " +
    "          ?, " +
    "          ?, " +
    "          ?, " +
    "          ? ) ");

  pstmt.setInt(1, 4);
  pstmt.setString(2, "DOE");
  pstmt.setString(3, "JOHN");
  pstmt.setDate(4,
    java.sql.Date.valueOf("1980-02-28"));
  pstmt.setString(5, "M");
  pstmt.addBatch();

  pstmt.setInt(1, 5);
  pstmt.setString(2, "DOE");
  pstmt.setString(3, "JANE");
  pstmt.setDate(4,
    java.sql.Date.valueOf("1980-01-01"));
  pstmt.setString(5, "F");
  pstmt.addBatch();

  pstmt.setInt(1, 6);
  pstmt.setString(2, "DOUGH");
  pstmt.setString(3, "PLAY");
  pstmt.setNull(4, Types.DATE);
  pstmt.setNull(5, Types.CHAR);
  pstmt.addBatch();

  int[] updateArray = pstmt.executeBatch();

  pstmt.close();
```

```
    pstmt = null;
    conn.commit();
  }
catch (SQLException e) {
    ...
  }
```

The updateArray is an array of int values, one for each SQL statement in the order they were added to the batch. If the int value for a statement is greater than or equal to 0, it may refer to the number of rows affected by the SQL statement. If the value is -2, the statement was successful, but the number of rows affected is unknown. A value of -3 means the statement failed. Be aware that some drivers continue to process statements when one fails, while other drivers do not; instead, they throw a BatchUpdateException, in which case you should roll back your batch.

Working with Large Objects

Large streaming SQL data types such as binary large objects (BLOBs) and character large objects (CLOBs) require you to use streams to move data between your program and the database efficiently. Since the difference between a BLOB and CLOB boils down to binary (byte) data versus character data, and, accordingly, the use of binary versus character streams, I'll only discuss the use of BLOBs here.

Inserting a BLOB

To insert a BLOB into a database, use PreparedStatement's setBinaryStream( ) method, passing it the column index, an InputStream, and the length of the object in bytes as follows (assuming a Connection, conn, already exists):

```
int              rows = 0;
PreparedStatement pstmt = null;
try {
  pstmt = conn.prepareStatement(
    "insert into PHOTOGRAPH ( " +
```

```
         "       person_id, " +
         "       pic ) " +
         "values ( " +
         "       ?, " +
         "       ? )");
       pstmt.setInt(1, 7);
       File file = new File("tim.gif");
       long fileLength = file.length();
       FileInputStream fis = new FileInputStream(file);
       pstmt.setBinaryStream(2, fis, (int)fileLength);
       rows = pstmt.executeUpdate();
       fis.close();
       pstmt.close();
       pstmt = null;
       conn.commit();
       }
   }
   catch (FileNotFoundException e) {
     ...
   }
   catch (IOException e) {
     ...
   }
   catch (SQLException e) {
     ...
   }
   finally {
     if (stmt != null)
       try { stmt.close(); } catch (Exception i) { }
   }
```

It's important that you close the input stream before you commit the SQL statement; otherwise, the data may not be saved.

Retrieving a BLOB

The accessors getBlob( ) and getClob( ) return a locator object (a pointer) to an actual BLOB or CLOB in the database. You use the locator's stream method, getBinaryStream( ) or getCharacterStream( ), to retrieve the large object from the database. Here's an example of retrieving a BLOB (assuming a Connection, conn, already exists):

```
Blob          blobLocator = null;
int                  rows = 0;
PreparedStatement pstmt = null;
try {
  rows = 0;
  pstmt = conn.prepareStatement(
    "select pic " +
    "from   PHOTOGRAPH " +
    "where  person_id = ? ");
  pstmt.setInt(1, 7);
  rset = pstmt.executeQuery( );
  if (rset.next( )) {
    rows++;
    // Get the locator from the database.
    Blob blobLocator = rset.getBlob(1);
    // Get a binary stream using the locator.
    InputStream is = blobLocator.getBinaryStream( );
    File file = new File("tim.gif");
    FileOutputStream fos =
      new FileOutputStream(file);
    // Read and write the data 32 bytes at a time.
    int length   = 0;
    int bufferSize = 32;
    byte[ ] buffer  = new byte[bufferSize];
    while ((length = is.read(buffer)) != -1) {
      fos.write(buffer, 0, length);
    }
    is.close( );
    fos.close( );
  }
  pstmt.close( );
  pstmt = null;
  conn.commit( );
}
catch (IOException e) {
  ...
}
catch (SQLException e) {
  ...
}
finally {
  if (stmt != null)
    try { stmt.close( ); } catch (Exception i) { }
}
```

User-Defined Data Types

User-defined data types (UDTs) bring the world of object-orientation to relational databases. Using UDTs you can create an object-relational database, or objectbase, in which an object model can be directly implemented in the persistence layer. To store and retrieve UDTs, you can either manipulate them as SQL STRUCTs and ARRAYs (which I will not show here), or you can define Java classes that are mapped to the SQL UDTs, which you then use to materialize the UDTs in your Java program.

Creating a Java Class for a UDT

Java classes that will be used to materialize a UDT need to implement the SQLData interface. Most databases that support UDTs also provide a tool to generate Java classes that implement SQLData. Implementing the SQLData interface consists of coding three methods. The first, getSQLTypeName( ), needs to return the fully qualified name of the UDT as it exists in the database. The second, readSQL( ), reads your class attributes from an SQLInput stream in the order they exist in the UDT. The third, writeSQL( ), writes the values of your class attributes onto the SQLOutput stream in the order they exit in the UDT. Here's an example of a hand-coded class that implements the SQLData interface for an object table PERSON:

```java
import java.io.*;
import java.sql.*;

/**
A mirror class to hold a copy of SCOTT.PERSON_TYPE
*/
public class Person
  implements SQLData, Serializable {

  private int          person_id;
  private String       last_name;
  private String       first_name;
```

```java
  private java.sql.Date birth_date;
  private String        gender;

  public Person() { }

  // SQLData interface
  public String getSQLTypeName()
   throws SQLException {
    return "SCOTT.PERSON_TYPE";
  }
  public void readSQL(SQLInput stream, String type)
   throws SQLException {
    person_id  = stream.readInt();
    last_name  = stream.readString();
    first_name = stream.readString();
    birth_date = stream.readDate();
    gender     = stream.readString();
  }
  public void writeSQL(SQLOutput stream)
   throws SQLException {
    stream.writeInt(person_id);
    stream.writeString(last_name);
    stream.writeString(first_name);
    stream.writeDate(birth_date);
    stream.writeString(gender);
  }
  // Accessors
  public Int getPersonId() {
    return person_id;
  }
  public String getLastName() {
    return last_name;
  }
  public String getFirstName() {
    return first_name;
  }
  public java.sql.Date getBirthDate() {
    return birth_date;
  }
  public String getGender() {
    return gender;
  }
  // Mutators
  public void setPersonId(int person_id) {
    this.person_id = person_id;
  }
```

```java
  public void setLastName(String last_name) {
    this.last_name = last_name;
  }
  public void setFirstName(String first_name) {
    this.first_name = first_name;
  }
  public void setBirthDate(
    java.sql.Date birth_date) {
    this.birth_date = birth_date;
  }
  public void setGender(String gender) {
    this.gender = gender;
  }
}
```

Updating a Type Map

Once you have a UDT and Java class to represent it, you
must update the Connection or PreparedStatement's type map
to let the driver know which class to materialize when you
retrieve a UDT from a database, and what kind of UDT to
materialize when you store the Java class in a database.
Updating a type map consists of retrieving the current type
map and adding the new mapping as in the following example (assuming a Connection, conn, already exists):

```java
try {
  java.util.Map map = conn.getTypeMap( );
  map.put(
    "SCOTT.PERSON_TYPE",
    Class.forName("Person"));
}
catch (ClassNotFoundException e) {
  ...
}
catch (SQLException e) {
  ...
}
```

Inserting a UDT

To insert a UDT, you start out by creating a new instance of
the class that represents it, setting attributes as necessary.

You then use PreparedStatement's setObject( ), passing the column index and new class instance. Since the type map has been updated, the JDBC driver knows which new instance of a database UDT to create. Here's an example that inserts a PERSON_TYPE instance into object table PERSON_OBJ_TAB (assuming a Connection, conn, already exists):

```
PreparedStatement pstmt = null;
try {
  // Create a new instance.
  Person person = new Person( );
  person.setPersonId(1);
  person.setLastName("DOE");
  person.setFirstName("JOHN");
  person.setBirthDate(
    java.sql.Date.valueOf("1980-02-28"));
  person.setGender("M");
  // Insert it into an object table.
  pstmt = conn.prepareStatement(
    "insert into PERSON_OBJ_TAB values ( ? )");
  pstmt.setObject(1, person);
  int rows = pstmt.executeUpdate( );
  pstmt.close( );
  pstmt = null;
  conn.commit( );
}
catch (SQLException e) {
  ...
}
finally {
  if (stmt != null)
    try { stmt.close( ); } catch (Exception i) { }
}
```

Selecting a UDT

To select a UDT, you start by formulating an SQL SELECT statement that returns a UDT as an object. Execute the SELECT statement, and then use the Statement, PreparedStatement, or CallableStatement's getObject( ) method, casting the object it returns to the appropriate Java class type. The driver uses its updated type map to determine which Java class to materialize for the selected UDT.

Here's an example that selects a UDT PERSON_TYPE from object table PERSON_OBJ_TAB (assuming a Connection, conn, already exists):

```
ResultSet rset = null;
Statement stmt = null;
try {
  stmt = conn.createStatement();
  // value() is Oracle's materialization function
  rset = stmt.executeQuery(
    "select value(p) from PERSON_OBJ_TAB p");
  while (rset.next()) {
    // Cast the object
    person = (Person)rset.getObject(1);
    ...
  }
  rset.close();
  rset = null;
  stmt.close();
  stmt = null;
}
catch (SQLException e) {
  ...
}
finally {
  if (rset != null)
    try { rset.close(); } catch (Exception i) { }
  if (stmt != null)
    try { stmt.close(); } catch (Exception i) { }
}
```

Row Sets

A RowSet is a disconnectable, client-side cached, all-in-one object that acts as a Connection, PreparedStatement, and ResultSet. At minimum, you specify connection parameters and a command (SQL SELECT statement). When you use its execute() method to execute the specified command, the RowSet retrieves the data from the database into a client-side cache, and then disconnects. RowSets are ideal for those so-many-lines-of-output-at-a-time web pages, because you can create the RowSet, store it in an HttpSession, and selectively choose which rows to access. Here's an example using Oracle's cached row set:

```
import oracle.jdbc.rowset.*;
RowSet rwst = new OracleCachedRowSet( );
try {
  rwst.setUrl(url);
  rwst.setUsername(user);
  rwst.setPassword(password);
  rwst.setCommand("select * from DUAL");
  rwst.setType(ResultSet.TYPE_SCROLL_INSENSITIVE);
  rwst.execute( );
  while (rwst.next( )) {
    ...
  }
  rwst.beforeFirst( );
  while (rwst.next( )) {
    ...
  }
  rwst.close( );
}
catch (SQLException e) {
  ...
}
finally {
  if (rwst != null)
    try { rwst.close( ); } catch (Exception i) { }
}
```

Escape Syntax

Escape syntax provides a means of writing SQL statements that are portable from one database to another. However, problems can arise in some drivers' lack of support for JDBC escape syntax. Regardless, using these escape syntaxes will improve the portability of your code.

Date

{ d 'YYYY-MM-DD' }

d   Identifies the escape syntax as a date

YYYY Four-digit year

MM   Two-digit month (01–12)

DD   Two-digit day (01–31)

Use this escape syntax to specify SQL DATE values. For example, the 29th day of February, 1980 would be escaped as {d '1980-02-29'}.

Time

{ t 'hh:mm:ss' }

t   Identifies the escape syntax as a time

hh   Two-digit hour (00–23)

mm   Two-digit minute (00–59)

ss   Two-digit second (00–59)

Use this escape syntax to specify SQL TIME values. For example, 6:31 P.M. would be escaped as {t '18:31:00'}.

Timestamp

{ ts 'YYYY-MM-DD hh:mm:ss.fff }

ts   Identifies the escape syntax as a timestamp

YYYY Four-digit year

MM   Two-digit month (01–12)

DD   Two-digit day (01–31)

hh   Two-digit hour (00–23)

mm   Two-digit minute (00–59)

ss   Two-digit second (00–59)

fff   Optional three-digit microseconds

Use this escape syntax to specify SQL TIMESTAMP or DATE and TIME values. 6:31 P.M. on the 29th day of February, 1980 would be escaped as {ts '1980-02-29 18:31:00'}.

Function

{ fn functionName }

Use this escape syntax to specify an ANSI SQL database function that should be mapped by the driver to the database's proprietary equivalent function.

Outer join

```
{ oj outerJoinClause }
```

Use this syntax to specify portable outer joins.

SQL LIKE

```
value1 LIKE value2 { escape 'character' }
```

Use this syntax to specify an escape character to be used to escape one of the SQL wildcard characters.

Stored procedure

```
{ call procedureName[( ?, ?, ...)] }
{ ? = call functionName[( ?, ?, ...)] }
```

Use this syntax to escape a stored procedure call. The first syntax is for stored procedures that do not return a value. The second syntax is for procedures that do return a value.

The square brackets ([ ]) indicate that what lies between them is optional. The question marks (?) are placeholders for IN, OUT, and IN/OUT parameters.

Transaction Management

By default, new connections are in autocommit mode. In autocommit mode, every SQL statement is committed immediately after it is executed. You can turn autocommit on or off by executing Connection's setAutoCommit( ) method. true turns autocommit on, while false turns it off. If autocommit is off, then you must manage transactions manually. To commit, execute Connection's commit( ) method. To roll back, execute Connection's rollback( ) method.

The JDBC API

This section of the book provides a quick reference to the JDBC API. Keep in mind as you go through the API that all

Java classes (not interfaces) inherit methods from java.lang. Object. Also, all Exceptions inherit methods from java.lang. Throwable.

Table 3 shows the relationship between versions of Java and the JDBC APIs.

Table 3. Java and JDBC versions

Java version	JDBC API version
1.1.x	JDBC 1.0
1.2.x	JDBC 2.1 Core and JDBC 2.0 Optional Package (OP)
1.3.x	Portions of JDBC 3.0
1.4.x	JDBC 3.0

In the heading for a class or interface, or after the description of a method, you'll find notes about when the class, interface, or method became available (e.g., Java 1.2). This note indicates that the class, interface, or method under discussion became available in Java 1.2. The absence of any version notes means the item is part of the JDBC 1.0 API.

Array   Java 1.2

Interface name: java.sql.Array

Array represents the SQL type ARRAY, which in turn represents a collection in SQL. All of its methods can throw an SQLException.

Methods

Object getArray( )
> Returns the corresponding SQL ARRAY value as a Java Array using the default type map.

Object getArray(long index, int count)
> Returns a portion of the corresponding SQL ARRAY value as a Java Array using the default type map, from index for count elements.

Object getArray(long index, int count, Map map)
> Returns a portion of the corresponding SQL ARRAY value as a Java Array using the specified type map, from index, for count elements.

Object getArray(Map map)
>   Returns the corresponding SQL ARRAY value as a Java Array using the specified type map.

int getBaseType( )
>   Returns a constant from the java.sql.Types class for the elements in this Array.

String getBaseTypeName( )
>   Returns the database-specific or UDT SQL type name for the elements in this Array.

ResultSet getResultSet( )
>   Returns the SQL ARRAY as a result set using the default type map.

ResultSet getResultSet(long index, int count)
>   Returns a portion of the corresponding SQL ARRAY as a result set using the default type map, from index for count elements.

ResultSet getResultSet(long index, int count, Map map)
>   Returns a portion of the corresponding SQL ARRAY as a result set using the specified type map, from index for count elements.

ResultSet getResultSet(Map map)
>   Returns the SQL ARRAY as a result set using the specified type map.

BatchUpdateException

Java 1.2

Class name: java.sql.BatchUpdateException

Extends java.sql.SQLException
Implements java.io.Serializable

BatchUpdateException is a batch operation–specific exception.

Constructors

```
BatchUpdateException( )
BatchUpdateException(int[ ] updateCounts)
BatchUpdateException(String reason, int[ ] updateCounts)
BatchUpdateException(String reason, String SQLState,
   int[ ] updateCounts)
BatchUpdateException(String reason, String SQLState,
   int vendorCode, int[ ] updateCounts)
```

Method

```
int[ ] getUpdateCounts( )
```
Returns an array of int with the number of rows affected, or -2 for success, or -3 for failure, for each SQL statement in the batch before this exception was thrown. (Java 1.3)

Methods inherited from java.sql.SQLException

```
int getErrorCode( )
SQLException getNextException( )
String getSQLState( )
void setNextException(SQLException ex)
```

Blob   Java 1.2

Interface name: java.sql.Blob

Blob is a locator data type that maps to an SQL Binary Large Object (BLOB). All of Blob's methods can throw an SQLException.

Methods

```
InputStream getBinaryStream( )
```
Returns an InputStream that retrieves the BLOB value from the database as a stream.

```
byte[ ] getBytes(long pos, int length)
```
Returns a specified portion of the BLOB value from the database as a byte array.

```
long length( )
```
Returns the length of the BLOB in the database in bytes.

```
long position(Blob pattern, long start)
```
Returns the first position of the BLOB pattern found in the BLOB value from the database starting at byte position start.

```
long position(byte[ ] pattern, long start)
```
Returns the first position of the byte array pattern found in the BLOB value from the database starting at byte position start.

```
OutputStream setBinaryStream(long position)
```
Returns an OutputStream that writes the BLOB value to the database as a stream at the specified starting position. (Java 1.4)

```
int setBytes(long position, byte[ ] bytes)
```
Writes the byte array to the BLOB value in the database, at the given starting position, and returns the number of bytes written. (Java 1.4)

```
int setBytes(long position, byte[] bytes, int offset, int
   length)
```
Writes the a portion of the byte array specified by offset and length to the BLOB value in the database at the given starting position, and returns the number of bytes written. (Java 1.4)

```
void truncate(long length)
```
Truncates the BLOB value to the specified length. (Java 1.4)

CallableStatement

Interface name: java.sql.CallableStatement   Extends java.sql.PreparedStatement

CallableStatement is an object used to execute SQL stored procedures. Use the following escape syntax for SQL function calls:

```
{? = call procedureName[( ?, ?, ...)]}
```

For procedure calls use:

```
{call procedureName[( ?, ?, ...)]}
```

The brackets ([ ]) denote optionality. All of CallableStatement's methods can throw an SQLException.

Fields inherited from Statement

```
static final int CLOSE_ALL_RESULTS
static final int CLOSE_CURRENT_RESULT
static final int EXECUTE_FAILED
static final int KEEP_CURRENT_RESULT
static final int NO_GENERATED_KEYS
static final int RETURN_GENERATED_KEYS
static final int SUCCESS_NO_INFO
```

Methods

NOTE

The following getXXX( ) methods get a stored procedure's parameter value (SQL OUT parameter) for the specified parameter index (starting from 1, incrementing left to right) or parameter name, and map that parameter value to the return data type.

```
Array getArray(int parameterIndex)
Array getArray(String parameterName)
```
Returns a value as an Array. (Java 1.2/1.4)

```
BigDecimal getBigDecimal(int parameterIndex)
BigDecimal getBigDecimal(String parameterName)
```
Returns a value as a java.math.BigDecimal. (Java 1.2/1.4)

```
Blob getBlob(int parameterIndex)
Blob getBlob(String parameterName)
```
Returns a Blob locator, not the BLOB value. Use the Blob's getBinaryStream( ) method to retrieve the BLOB value using an InputStream, or use its setBinaryStream( ) method to write the BLOB value using an OutputStream. (Java 1.2/1.4)

```
boolean getBoolean(int parameterIndex)
boolean getBoolean(String parameterName)
```
Returns a value as a boolean. (Java 1.4)

```
byte getByte(int parameterIndex)
byte getByte(String parameterName)
```
Returns a value as a byte. (Java 1.4)

```
byte[ ] getBytes(int parameterIndex)
byte[ ] getBytes(String parameterName)
```
Returns a value as a byte array. (Java 1.4)

```
Clob getClob(int parameterIndex)
Clob getClob(String parameterName)
```
Returns a Clob locator, not the CLOB value. Use the Clob's getCharacterStream( ) method to retrieve the CLOB value using a Reader, or use its setCharacterStream( ) method to write the CLOB value using a Writer. (Java 1.2/1.4)

```
Date getDate(int parameterIndex)
Date getDate(String parameterName)
```
Returns a value as a java.sql.Date. (Java 1.4)

```
Date getDate(int parameterIndex, Calendar calendar)
```
Returns the value as a java.sql.Date for the specified Calendar. (Java 1.2/1.4)

```
double getDouble(int parameterIndex)
double getDouble(String parameterName)
```
Returns the value as a double. (Java 1.4)

```
float getFloat(int parameterIndex)
float getFloat(String parameterName)
```
Returns a value as a float. (Java 1.4)

```
int getInt(int parameterIndex)
int getInt(String parameterName)
```
Returns a value as an int. (Java 1.4)

```
long getLong(int parameterIndex)
long getLong(String parameterName)
```
Returns a value as a long. (Java 1.4)

```
Object getObject(int parameterIndex)
Object getObject(String parameterName)
```
Returns a value as an Object. (Java 1.4)

```
Object getObject(int parameterIndex, Map map)
Object getObject(String parameterName, Map map)
```
Returns a user-defined type (UDT) using the specified type map as an Object. (Java 1.2/1.4)

```
Ref getRef(int parameterIndex)
Ref getRef(String parameterName)
```
Returns a value as a Ref. (Java 1.2/1.4)

```
short getShort(int parameterIndex)
short getShort(String parameterName)
```
Returns a value as a short. (Java 1.4)

```
String getString(int parameterIndex)
String getString(String parameterName)
```
Returns a value as a String. (Java 1.4)

```
Time getTime(int parameterIndex)
Time getTime(String parameterName)
```
Returns a value as a Time. (Java 1.4)

```
Time getTime(int parameterIndex, Calendar calendar)
Time getTime(String parameterName, Calendar calendar)
```
Returns a value as a Time using the specified Calendar. (Java 1.2/1.4)

```
Timestamp getTimestamp(int parameterIndex)
Timestamp getTimestamp(String parameterName)
```
Returns a value as a Timestamp. (Java 1.4)

```
Timestamp getTimestamp(int parameterIndex, Calendar calendar)
Timestamp getTimestamp(String parameterName,
  Calendar calendar)
```
Returns a value as a Timestamp using the specified Calendar. (Java 1.2/1.4)

```
URL getURL(int parameterIndex)
URL getURL(String parameterName)
```
Returns a value as a java.net.URL. (Java 1.4)

```
void registerOutParameter(int parameterIndex, int sqlType)
void registerOutParameter(String parameterName, int sqlType)
```
> Registers an SQL OUT parameter at the specified parameter index (starting with 1 and incrementing from left to right) to the java.sql.Types constant. (Java 1.4)

```
void registerOutParameter(int parameterIndex, int sqlType,
  int scale)
void registerOutParameter(String parameterName, int sqlType,
  int scale)
```
> Registers an SQL OUT parameter at the specified parameter index (starting with 1 and incrementing from left to right) to the java.sql.Types constant, with the specified precision. (Java 1.4)

```
void registerOutParameter(int parameterIndex, int sqlType,
  String typeName)
void registerOutParameter(String parameterName, int sqlType,
  String typeName)
```
> Registers an SQL OUT parameter at the specified parameter index (starting with 1 and incrementing from left to right) to the java.sql.Types constant, and user-defined type (UDT). (Java 1.2/1.4)

```
void setAsciiStream(String parameterName, InputStream x,
  int length)
```
> Sets a value using the first length bytes of the specified input stream. (Java 1.4)

```
void setBigDecimal(String parameterName, BigDecimal x)
```
> Sets a value using the specified java.math.BigDecimal. (Java 1.4)

```
void setBinaryStream(String parameterName, InputStream x,
  int length)
```
> Sets a value using the first length bytes of the specified input stream. (Java 1.4)

```
void setBoolean(String parameterName, boolean x)
```
> Sets a value using the specified boolean. (Java 1.4)

```
void setByte(String parameterName, byte x)
```
> Sets a value using the specified byte. (Java 1.4)

```
void setBytes(String parameterName, byte[ ] x)
```
> Sets a value using the specified byte array. (Java 1.4)

void setCharacterStream(String parameterName, Reader reader,
  int length)
> Sets a value using the first length characters of the specified
> reader. (Java 1.4)

void setDate(String parameterName, Date x)
> Sets a value using the specified java.sql.Date. (Java 1.4)

void setDate(String parameterName, Date x, Calendar calendar)
> Sets a value using the specified java.sql.Date and Calendar.
> (Java 1.4)

void setDouble(String parameterName, double x)
> Sets a value using the specified double. (Java 1.4)

void setFloat(String parameterName, float x)
> Sets a value using the specified float. (Java 1.4)

void setInt(String parameterName, int x)
> Sets a value using the specified int. (Java 1.4)

void setLong(String parameterName, long x)
> Sets a value using the specified long. (Java 1.4)

void setNull(String parameterName, int sqlType)
> Sets the specified parameter to an SQL NULL value for the
> specified java.sql.Types constant. (Java 1.4)

void setNull(String parameterName, int sqlType,
  String typeName)
> Sets the specified parameter to an SQL NULL value for the
> specified user-defined type (UDT). (Java 1.4)

void setObject(String parameterName, Object x)
> Sets the value using the specified Object. (Java 1.4)

void setObject(String parameterName, Object x, int sqlType)
> Sets a value using the specified Object and java.sql.Types
> constant. (Java 1.4)

void setObject(String parameterName, Object x, int sqlType,
  int scale)
> Sets a value using the specified Object, java.sql.Types
> constant, and scale (for numeric data types). (Java 1.4)

void setShort(String parameterName, short x)
> Sets a value using the specified short. (Java 1.4)

void setString(String parameterName, String x)
> Sets a value using the specified String. (Java 1.4)

void setTime(String parameterName, Time x)
    Sets a value using the specified Time. (Java 1.4)

void setTime(String parameterName, Time x, Calendar calendar)
    Sets a value using the specified Time and Calendar. (Java 1.4)

void setTimestamp(String parameterName, Timestamp x)
    Sets a value using the specified Timestamp. (Java 1.4)

void setTimestamp(String parameterName, Timestamp x,
  Calendar calendar)
    Sets a value using the specified Timestamp and Calendar. (Java
    1.4)

void setURL(String parameterName, URL val)
    Sets a value using the specified java.net.URL. (Java 1.4)

boolean wasNull( )
    Returns true if the last accessor method called encountered
    an SQL NULL value.

Methods inherited from java.sql.PreparedStatement

```
void addBatch( )
void clearParameters( )
boolean execute( )
ResultSet executeQuery( )
int executeUpdate( )
ResultSetMetaData getMetaData( )
ParameterMetaData getParameterMetaData( )
void setArray(int parameterIndex, Array x)
void setAsciiStream(int parameterIndex, InputStream x,
   int length)
void setBigDecimal(int parameterIndex, BigDecimal x)
void setBinaryStream(int parameterIndex, InputStream x,
   int length)
void setBlob(int parameterIndex, Blob x)
void setBoolean(int parameterIndex, boolean x)
void setByte(int parameterIndex, byte x)
void setBytes(int parameterIndex, byte[ ] x)
void setCharacterStream(int parameterIndex, Reader reader,
   int length)
void setClob(int parameterIndex, Clob x)
void setDate(int parameterIndex, java.sql.Date x)
void setDate(int parameterIndex, java.sql.Date x,
   Calendar calendar)
void setDouble(int parameterIndex, double x)
void setFloat(int parameterIndex, float x)
```

```
void setInt(int parameterIndex, int x)
void setLong(int parameterIndex, long x)
void setNull(int parameterIndex, int sqlType)
void setNull(int parameterIndex, int sqlType, String typeName)
void setObject(int parameterIndex, Object x)
void setObject(int parameterIndex,Object x,int sqlType)
void setObject(int parameterIndex, Object x int sqlType,
    int scale)
void setRef(int parameterIndex, Ref x)
void setShort(int parameterIndex, short x)
void setString(int parameterIndex, String x)
void setTime(int parameterIndex, java.sql.Time x)
void setTime(int parameterIndex, java.sql.Time x,
    Calendar calendar)
void setTimestamp(int parameterIndex, Timestamp x)
void setTimestamp(int parameterIndex, Timestamp x,
    Calendar calendar)
void setURL(int parameterIndex, URL x)
```

Methods inherited from java.sql.Statement

```
void addBatch(String sql)
void cancel( )
void clearBatch( )
void clearWarnings( )
void close( )
boolean execute(String sql)
boolean execute(String sql, int autoGeneratedKeys)
boolean execute(String sql, int[ ] columnIndexes)
boolean execute(String sql, String[ ] columnNames)
int[ ] executeBatch( )
ResultSet executeQuery(String sql)
int executeUpdate(String sql)
int executeUpdate(String sql, int autoGeneratedKeys)
int executeUpdate(String sql, int[ ] columnIndexes)
int executeUpdate(String sql, String[ ] columnNames)
Connection getConnection( )
int getFetchDirection( )
int getFetchSize( )
ResultSet getGeneratedKeys( )
int getMaxFieldSize( )
int getMaxRows( )
boolean getMoreResults( )
boolean getMoreResults(int current)
int getQueryTimeout( )
ResultSet getResultSet( )
```

```
int getResultSetConcurrency( )
int getResultSetHoldability( )
int getResultSetType( )
int getUpdateCount( )
SQLWarning getWarnings( )
void setCursorName(String name)
void setEscapeProcessing(boolean enable)
void setFetchDirection(int direction)
void setFetchSize(int rows)
void setMaxFieldSize(int max)
void setMaxRows(int max)
void setQueryTimeout(int seconds)
```

Clob   Java 1.2

Interface name: java.sql.Clob

Clob is a locator type that maps to an SQL Character Large Object (CLOB). All of Clob's methods can throw an SQLException.

Methods

InputStream getAsciiStream( )
> Returns an InputStream that will retrieve the CLOB value from the database as an ASCII stream.

Reader getCharacterStream( )
> Returns a Reader that will retrieve the CLOB value from the database as a Unicode stream.

String getSubString(long pos, int length)
> Returns a specified portion of the CLOB value from the database as a string.

long length( )
> Returns the length of the CLOB in the database in characters.

long position(Clob pattern, long start)
> Returns the first position of CLOB, pattern, found in this CLOB value from the database, starting at character position start.

long position(String pattern, long start)
> Returns the first position of string, pattern, found in this CLOB value from the database, starting at character position start.

OutputStream setAsciiStream(long position)
>   Returns an AsciiStream to be used to write the CLOB value to the database as an ASCII stream, starting at the specified position. (Java 1.4)

Writer setCharacterStream(long position)
>   Returns a Writer that will write the CLOB value to the database as a Unicode stream, starting at the specified position. (Java 1.4)

int setString(long position, String string)
>   Writes the specified string to the CLOB value in the database starting at the given position, and returns the number of characters written. (Java 1.4)

int setString(long position, String string, int offset,
  int length)
>   Writes the substring specified by offset and length to the CLOB value in the database starting at the given position, and returns the number of characters written. (Java 1.4)

void truncate(long length)
>   Truncates the CLOB value to the specified length. (Java 1.4)

Connection

Interface name: java.sql.Connection

Connection represents a session with a specific database. Use this object to get a Statement to execute a dynamic SQL statement, a PreparedStatement to execute a precompiled SQL statement, a CallableStatement to execute a stored procedure, or DatabaseMetaData to determine a database's capabilities. All of Connection's methods can throw an SQLException.

Fields

static final int TRANSACTION_NONE
>   Transactions are not supported by this database.

static final int TRANSACTION_READ_COMMITTED
>   Dirty reads are prevented; nonrepeatable reads and phantom reads can occur.

static final int TRANSACTION_READ_UNCOMMITTED
>   Dirty reads, nonrepeatable reads, and phantom reads can occur.

```
static final int TRANSACTION_REPEATABLE_READ
```
Dirty reads and nonrepeatable reads are prevented; phantom reads can occur.

```
static final int TRANSACTION_SERIALIZABLE
```
Dirty reads, nonrepeatable reads, and phantom reads are prevented.

Methods

```
void clearWarnings()
```
Clears any SQL warnings for this connection.

```
void close()
```
Closes the connection to the database and immediately releases any JDBC resources.

```
void commit()
```
Commits the current database transaction.

```
Statement createStatement()
```
Returns a Statement object, which can be used to execute dynamic SQL statements.

```
Statement createStatement(int resultSetType,
  int resultSetConcurrency)
```
Returns a Statement object, which can be used to execute dynamic SQL statements with one of the following result set types (Java 1.2):

```
ResultSet.TYPE_FORWARD_ONLY
ResultSet.TYPE_SCROLL_INSENSITIVE
ResultSet.TYPE_SCROLL_SENSITIVE
```

and with one of the following concurrency settings:

```
ResultSet.CONCUR_READ_ONLY
ResultSet.CONCUR_UPDATABLE
```

```
Statement createStatement(int resultSetType,
  int resultSetConcurrency, int resultSetHoldability)
```
Returns a Statement object, which can be used to execute dynamic SQL statements with one of the following result set types (Java 1.4):

```
ResultSet.TYPE_FORWARD_ONLY
ResultSet.TYPE_SCROLL_INSENSITIVE
ResultSet.TYPE_SCROLL_SENSITIVE
```

one of the following concurrency settings:

```
ResultSet.CONCUR_READ_ONLY
ResultSet.CONCUR_UPDATABLE
```

and one of the following holdability settings:

```
ResultSet.CLOSE_CURSORS_AT_COMMIT
ResultSet.HOLD_CURSORS_OVER_COMMIT
```

boolean getAutoCommit( )

Returns the current autocommit mode.

String getCatalog( )

Returns the connection's catalog name.

int getHoldability( )

Returns the holdability setting for result sets created using this connection, which will match one the following constants (Java 1.4):

```
ResultSet.CLOSE_CURSORS_AT_COMMIT
ResultSet.HOLD_CURSORS_OVER_COMMIT
```

DatabaseMetaData getMetaData( )

Returns a database metadata object, which can be used to determine this database's capabilities.

int getTransactionIsolation( )

Returns the connection's transaction isolation level, which will match one of the following constants:

```
TRANSACTION_NONE
TRANSACTION_READ_COMMITTED
TRANSACTION_READ_UNCOMMITTED
TRANSACTION_REPEATABLE_READ
TRANSACTION_SERIALIZABLE
```

Map getTypeMap( )

Returns the connection's type map object. A type map object is used to map a database user-defined type (UDT) to a custom Java class. (Java 1.2)

SQLWarning getWarnings( )

Returns the first SQL warning, if any, for the connection; otherwise null.

boolean isClosed( )

Returns true if the connection is closed; otherwise false.

boolean isReadOnly( )

Returns true if the connection is in read-only mode; otherwise false.

String nativeSQL(String sql)

Returns the specified SQL statement in the database's native SQL grammar.

CallableStatement prepareCall(String sql)

Returns a CallableStatement object, which can be used to execute stored procedures.

CallableStatement prepareCall(String sql, int resultSetType, int resultSetConcurrency)

Returns a CallableStatement object, which can be used to execute stored procedures with the specified result set type (Java 1.2):

```
ResultSet.TYPE_FORWARD_ONLY
ResultSet.TYPE_SCROLL_INSENSITIVE
ResultSet.TYPE_SCROLL_SENSITIVE
```

and result set concurrency:

```
ResultSet.CONCUR_READ_ONLY
ResultSet.CONCUR_UPDATABLE
```

CallableStatement prepareCall(String sql, int resultSetType, int resultSetConcurrency, int resultSetHoldability)

Returns a CallableStatement object, which can be used to execute stored procedures with the specified result set type (Java 1.4):

```
ResultSet.TYPE_FORWARD_ONLY
ResultSet.TYPE_SCROLL_INSENSITIVE
ResultSet.TYPE_SCROLL_SENSITIVE
```

result set concurrency:

```
ResultSet.CONCUR_READ_ONLY
ResultSet.CONCUR_UPDATABLE
```

and result set holdability:

```
ResultSet.CLOSE_CURSORS_AT_COMMIT
ResultSet.HOLD_CURSORS_OVER_COMMIT
```

PreparedStatement prepareStatement(String sql)

Returns a PreparedStatement object, which can be used to precompile and execute SQL INSERT, UPDATE, DELETE, and SELECT statements.

PreparedStatement prepareStatement(String sql, int autoGeneratedKeys)

Returns a PreparedStatement object that can retrieve auto-generated keys, and which can be used to precompile and execute SQL INSERT, UPDATE, DELETE, and SELECT statements. (Java 1.4)

PreparedStatement prepareStatement(String sql,
  int resultSetType, int resultSetConcurrency)

Returns a PreparedStatement object, which can be used to precompile and execute SQL INSERT, UPDATE, DELETE, and SELECT statements with the specified result set type (Java 1.2):

```
ResultSet.TYPE_FORWARD_ONLY
ResultSet.TYPE_SCROLL_INSENSITIVE
ResultSet.TYPE_SCROLL_SENSITIVE
```

and result set concurrency:

```
ResultSet.CONCUR_READ_ONLY
ResultSet.CONCUR_UPDATABLE
```

PreparedStatement prepareStatement(String sql,
  int resultSetType, int resultSetConcurrency,
  int resultSetHoldability)

Returns a PreparedStatement object, which can be used to precompile and execute SQL INSERT, UPDATE, DELETE, and SELECT statements with the specified result set type (Java 1.4):

```
ResultSet.TYPE_FORWARD_ONLY
ResultSet.TYPE_SCROLL_INSENSITIVE
ResultSet.TYPE_SCROLL_SENSITIVE
```

result set concurrency:

```
ResultSet.CONCUR_READ_ONLY
ResultSet.CONCUR_UPDATABLE
```

and result set holdability:

```
ResultSet.CLOSE_CURSORS_AT_COMMIT
ResultSet.HOLD_CURSORS_OVER_COMMIT
```

PreparedStatement prepareStatement(String sql,
  int[ ] columnIndexes)

PreparedStatement prepareStatement(String sql,
  String[ ] columnNames)

Returns a PreparedStatement object that can retrieve the auto-generated keys for the specified columns, which can be used to precompile and execute SQL INSERT, UPDATE, DELETE, and SELECT statements. (Java 1.4) `void releaseSavepoint(Savepoint savepoint)`

Releases the specified Savepoint from the current database transaction. (Java 1.4)

`void rollback( )`

Rolls back the current database transaction.

`void rollback(Savepoint savepoint)`

Rolls back the current database transaction to the specified Savepoint. (Java 1.4)

`void setAutoCommit(boolean autoCommit)`

Sets this connection's current autocommit mode.

`void setCatalog(String catalog)`

Sets this connection's catalog name to work with a subspace in the database.

`void setHoldability(int holdability)`

Sets the holdability for result sets created using this connection to one the following constants (Java 1.4):

```
ResultSet.CLOSE_CURSORS_AT_COMMIT
ResultSet.HOLD_CURSORS_OVER_COMMIT
```

`void setReadOnly(boolean readOnly)`

Sets the connection to read-only mode as a hint to the database to use optimizations.

`Savepoint setSavepoint( )`

Sets and returns an unnamed savepoint in the current database transaction. (Java 1.4)

`Savepoint setSavepoint(String name)`

Sets and returns a savepoint with the specified name in the current database transaction. (Java 1.4)

`void setTransactionIsolation(int level)`

Sets the transaction isolation level to the specified constant:

```
TRANSACTION_READ_COMMITTED
TRANSACTION_READ_UNCOMMITTED
TRANSACTION_REPEATABLE_READ
TRANSACTION_SERIALIZABLE
```

Use DatabaseMetaData's supportsTransactionIsolationLevel( ) to determine if it is possible to set the transaction isolation level to a particular level first.

```
void setTypeMap(Map map)
```
Sets the connection's type map, which in turn becomes the default type map for subsequently created Statement, PreparedStatement, or CallableStatement objects. (Java 1.2)

ConnectionEvent

Java 1.4, JDBC 2.0 OP

Class name: javax.sql.ConnectionEvent | Extends java.util.EventObject

ConnectionEvent is a connection-specific event object.

Constructors

```
ConnectionEvent(PooledConnection con)
ConnectionEvent(PooledConnection con, SQLException ex)
```

Method

```
SQLException getSQLException( )
```
Returns the SQL exception that is about to be thrown.

Methods inherited from java.util.EventObject

```
Object getSource( )
String toString( )
```

ConnectionEventListener

Java 1.4, JDBC 2.0 OP

Interface name: javax.sql.ConnectionEventListener | Extends java.util.EventListener

The ConnectionEventListener interface is implemented by any object that wants to register to receive events generated by a pooled connection.

Methods

```
void connectionClosed(ConnectionEvent event)
```
Executed whenever a pooled connection object's close( ) method is executed.

```
void connectionErrorOccurred(ConnectionEvent event)
```
Executed whenever a pooled connection object encounters a fatal error, just before it throws an SQL exception.

ConnectionPoolDataSource

Interface name: javax.sql.ConnectionPoolDataSource

ConnectionPoolDataSource is a factory for pooled connections. A connection pool data source is typically retrieved via JNDI. All of its methods can throw an SQLException.

Methods

int getLoginTimeout( )
> Returns the maximum amount of time the data source will wait while establishing a connection, in seconds.

PrintWriter getLogWriter( )
> Returns the log writer for the data source.

PooledConnection getPooledConnection( )
> Returns a pooled connection.

PooledConnection getPooledConnection(String user,
  String password)
> Returns a pooled connection using the specified user and password for authentication.

void setLoginTimeout(int seconds)
> Sets the maximum amount of time the data source will wait while establishing a connection, in seconds.

void setLogWriter(PrintWriter out)
> Sets the log writer for the data source.

DatabaseMetaData

Interface name: java.sql.DatabaseMetaData

DatabaseMetaData is used to determine the capabilities of a JDBC driver and its database. If a given method of this interface is not supported by a JDBC driver, the method will either throw an SQLException, or in the case of a method that returns a result set, it may return null. Some methods take search patterns as arguments. The pattern values used can be the SQL wildcard characters % and _. Other search arguments accept an empty set ("") when the argument is not applicable, or null to drop the argument from the search criteria. All of its methods can throw an SQLException.

Fields

static int attributeNoNulls
  The attribute is not nullable.

static int attributeNullable
  The attribute is nullable.

static int attributeNullableUnknown
  The nullability of the attribute is unknown.

static int bestRowNotPseudo
  The best row identifier is not a pseudo column.

static int bestRowPseudo
  The best row identifier is a pseudo column.

static int bestRowSession
  The scope of the best row identifier is the current session.

static int bestRowTemporary
  The scope of the best row identifier lasts only while the row is
  being used.

static int bestRowTransaction
  The scope of the best row identifier is the current transaction.

static int bestRowUnknown
  The best row identifier may or may not be a pseudo column.

static int columnNoNulls
  The column is not nullable.

static int columnNullable
  The column is nullable.

static int columnNullableUnknown
  The nullability of columns is unknown.

static int importedKeyCascade
  Actions related to foreign keys will be cascaded.

static int importedKeyInitiallyDeferred
  Actions related to foreign keys will be deferred.

static int importedKeyInitiallyImmediate
  Actions related to foreign keys will be immediate.

static int importedKeyNoAction
  No actions related to foreign keys will be taken.

static int importedKeyNotDeferrable
  Actions related to foreign keys are not deferrable.

```
static int importedKeyRestrict
```
Actions related to foreign keys are restricted.

```
static int importedKeySetDefault
```
Actions related to foreign keys will use default values.

```
static int importedKeySetNull
```
Actions related to foreign key will use NULL values.

```
static int procedureColumnIn
```
The stored procedure column passes IN parameters.

```
static int procedureColumnInOut
```
The stored procedure column passes IN OUT parameters.

```
static int procedureColumnOut
```
The stored procedure column passes OUT parameters.

```
static int procedureColumnResult
```
The stored procedure column passes a result set.

```
static int procedureColumnReturn
```
The stored procedure column passes return values.

```
static int procedureColumnUnknown
```
The purpose of the stored procedure column is unknown.

```
static int procedureNoNulls
```
In the stored procedure column, NULL values are not allowed.

```
static int procedureNoResult
```
The stored procedure does not return a result.

```
static int procedureNullable
```
In the stored procedure column, NULL values are allowed.

```
static int procedureNullableUnknown
```
In the stored procedure column, nullability is unknown.

```
static int procedureResultUnknown
```
Whether the stored procedure returns a value or result set is unknown.

```
static int procedureReturnsResult
```
The stored procedure returns a result value of a result set.

```
static int sqlStateSQL99
```
The value is an SQL99 SQLSTATE.

```
static int sqlStateXOpen
```
The value is an X/Open SQL CLI SQLSTATE.

static short `tableIndexClustered`
The table index is clustered.

static short `tableIndexHashed`
The table index is hashed.

static short `tableIndexOther`
The table index is of some unknown type.

static short `tableIndexStatistic`
The table index is statistical.

static int `typeNoNulls`
The column/parameter may not be NULL.

static int `typeNullable`
The column/parameter may be NULL.

static int `typeNullableUnknown`
The column/parameter nullability is unknown.

static int `typePredBasic`
This column can be used only in a WHERE clause without the keyword LIKE.

static int `typePredChar`
This column can only be used in a WHERE clause with the keyword LIKE.

static int `typePredNone`
This column cannot be used in a WHERE clause.

static int `typeSearchable`
This column can be used in any WHERE clause.

static int `versionColumnNotPseudo`
The versioning column is not a pseudo column.

static int `versionColumnPseudo`
The versioning column is a pseudo column.

static int `versionColumnUnknown`
The versioning column may or may not be a pseudo column.

Methods

boolean `allProceduresAreCallable( )`
Returns true if the current user can execute all the procedures returned by getProcedures( ).

boolean allTablesAreSelectable( )
>   Returns true if the current user can SELECT all the tables returned by getTables( ).

boolean dataDefinitionCausesTransactionCommit( )
>   Returns true if DDL execution forces a commit.

boolean dataDefinitionIgnoredInTransactions( )
>   Returns true if DDL execution is ignored by a transaction.

boolean deletesAreDetected(int type)
>   Returns true if ResultSet's rowDeleted( ) can detect a deleted row. (Java 1.2)

boolean doesMaxRowSizeIncludeBlobs( )
>   Returns true if getMaxRowSize( ) includes LONGVARCHAR and LONGVARBINARY.

ResultSet getAttributes(String catalog, String schemaPattern, String typeNamePattern, String attributeNamePattern)
>   Returns a result set that describes the specified UDT and attribute. The result set is defined as follows (Java 1.4):

>   TYPE_CAT
>>   A String value of the type's catalog name (may be null)

>   TYPE_SCHEM
>>   A String value of the type's schema name (may be null)

>   TYPE_NAME
>>   A String value of the type's name

>   ATTR_NAME
>>   A String value of the attribute's name

>   DATA_TYPE
>>   An int from java.sql.Types

>   ATTR_TYPE_NAME
>>   A String value of the data source's dependent type name

>   ATTR_SIZE
>>   An int value that describes the maximum number of characters or precision for a numeric type

>   DECIMAL_DIGITS
>>   An int value that describes the number of fractional digits for a numeric type

>   NUM_PREC_RADIX
>>   An int value that describes the radix (typically either 10 or 2)

NULLABLE
> An int value that describes whether the attribute is nullable; it will be one of these constants:
>
> ```
> attributeNoNulls
> attributeNullable
> attributeNullableUnknown
> ```

REMARKS
> A String value that is a comment describing the column (may be null)

ATTR_DEF
> A String value that describes the attribute's default value (may be null)

SQL_DATA_TYPE
> An int value that is not used in this method

SQL_DATETIME_SUB
> An int value that is not used in this method

CHAR_OCTET_LENGTH
> An int value that describes the maximum number of bytes in the attribute for character data types

ORDINAL_POSITION
> An int value that describes the ordinal position of the attribute in the type (starting from 1)

IS_NULLABLE
> A String value that describes the nullability. NO means it is definitely not nullable. YES means it may be nullable. An empty string means the nullability is unknown.

SCOPE_CATALOG
> The catalog name, as a String value, of the table that is the scope of a reference attribute (null if it isn't a REF)

SCOPE_SCHEMA
> The schema name, as a String value, of the table that is the scope of a reference attribute (null if it isn't a REF)

SCOPE_TABLE
> A String value of the table name that is the scope of a reference attribute (null if it isn't a REF)

SOURCE_DATA_TYPE
> A short that defines the source type from java.sql.Types (null if it isn't DISTINCT or REF) (Java 1.4)

ResultSet getBestRowIdentifier(String catalog, String schema,
  String table, int scope, boolean nullable)

Returns a result set that defines which columns best uniquely identify a row. The result set is defined as follows:

SCOPE
> A short value that describes the actual scope of the result. It is one of the following constants:
>
>> bestRowTemporary
>> bestRowTransaction
>> bestRowSession

COLUMN_NAME
> The column name as a String

DATA_TYPE
> A short from java.sql.Types

TYPE_NAME
> The database-dependent name, or user-defined type (UDT) name, as a String value

COLUMN_SIZE
> An int value that describes the precision of the data type

BUFFER_LENGTH
> An int value that is not used in this method

DECIMAL_DIGITS
> A short value that describes the scale of the data type

PSEUDO_COLUMN
> A short value that indicates whether or not the column is a pseudo column. It is one of the following constants:
>
>> bestRowUnknown
>> bestRowNotPseudo
>> bestRowPseudo

ResultSet getCatalogs( )

Returns a result set with one column, a String value that lists the catalog names.

String getCatalogSeparator( )

Returns the separator used between catalog and table name.

String getCatalogTerm( )

Returns the database's term for "catalog."

ResultSet getColumnPrivileges(String catalog, String schema,
  String table, String columnNamePattern)

Returns a result set that describes the access rights for a table's columns. The result set is defined as follows:

TABLE_CAT
> The catalog's name as a String value (may be null)

TABLE_SCHEM
> A String value of the schema's name (may be null)

TABLE_NAME
> A String value of the table's name

COLUMN_NAME
> A String value of the column's name

GRANTOR
> A String value showing the grantor of access to the column (may be null)

GRANTEE
> A String value showing the grantee of access

PRIVILEGE
> A String value that describes the type of access: SELECT, INSERT, UPDATE, REFERENCES, etc.

IS_GRANTABLE
> A String value of YES if the grantee may grant others privileges, NO otherwise, or null if this is unknown

ResultSet getColumns(String catalog, String schemaPattern,
  String tableNamePattern, String columnNamePattern)

Returns a result set that describes a table's columns. The result set is defined as follows:

TABLE_CAT
> A String value of the catalog name (may be null)

TABLE_SCHEM
> A String value of the schema name (may be null)

TABLE_NAME
> A String value of the table name

COLUMN_NAME
> A String value of the column name

DATA_TYPE
> A short from java.sql.Types

TYPE_NAME
> A String value of the database-dependent name, or of the user-defined type (UDT) name

COLUMN_SIZE
> An int value that describes the precision of the data type

BUFFER_LENGTH
> An int value that is not used in this method

DECIMAL_DIGITS
> An int value that describes the number of fractional digits

NUM_PREC_RADIX
> An int value that describes the radix (typically either 10 or 2)

NULLABLE
> One of the following int constants that describe whether the column is nullable:
>
>> columnNoNulls
>> columnNullable
>> columnNullableUnknown

REMARKS
> A String value that is a comment describing the column (may be null)

COLUMN_DEF
> A String value that describes a column's default value (may be null)

SQL_DATA_TYPE
> An int value that is not used in this method

SQL_DATETIME_SUB
> An int value that is not used in this method

CHAR_OCTET_LENGTH
> An int value that describes the maximum number of bytes in the column for character data types

ORDINAL_POSITION
> An int value that describes the ordinal position of the column in the table (starting from 1)

IS_NULLABLE
> A String value that describes the nullability. NO means it is definitely not nullable. YES means it may be nullable. An empty string means the nullability is unknown.

SCOPE_CATALOG
> A String value of the catalog of the table that is the scope of a reference attribute (null if it isn't a REF) (Java 1.4)

SCOPE_SCHEMA
> A String value of the schema of the table that is the scope of a reference attribute (null if it isn't a REF) (Java 1.4)

SCOPE_TABLE
> A String value of the table name that is the scope of a reference attribute (null if it isn't a REF) (Java 1.4)

SOURCE_DATA_TYPE
> A short that defines the source type from java.sql.Types (null if it isn't DISTINCT or REF) (Java 1.4)

Connection getConnection( )
> Returns this database metadata's connection. (Java 1.2)

ResultSet getCrossReference(String primaryKeyCatalog,
  String primaryKeySchema, String primaryKeyTable,
  String foreignKeyCatalog, String foreignKeySchema,
  String foreignKeyTable)
> Returns a result set that describes the foreign key relationship between the two specified tables. The result set is defined as follows:

PKTABLE_CAT
> A String value of the primary key catalog name (may be null)

PKTABLE_SCHEM
> A String value of the primary key schema name (may be null)

PKTABLE_NAME
> A String value of the primary key table name

PKCOLUMN_NAME
> A String value of the primary key column name

FKTABLE_CAT
> A String value of the foreign key catalog name (may be null)

FKTABLE_SCHEM
> A String value of the foreign key schema name (may be null)

FKTABLE_NAME
A String value of the foreign key table name

FKCOLUMN_NAME
A String value of the primary key column name

KEY_SEQ
A short value that is the sequence number of the column within the foreign key

UPDATE_RULE
A short constant that describes what happens to the foreign key when the primary key is updated:

    importedKeyNoAction
    importedKeyCascade
    importedKeySetNull
    importedKeySetDefault
    importedKeyRestrict

DELETE_RULE
A short constant that describes what happens to the foreign key when the primary key is deleted:

    importedKeyNoAction
    importedKeyCascade
    importedKeySetNull
    importedKeySetDefault
    importedKeyRestrict

FK_NAME
A String value of the foreign key name (may be null)

PK_NAME
A String value of the primary key name (may be null)

DEFERRABILITY
A short constant that describes whether the evaluation of the foreign key constraints can be deferred until the transaction is committed. It can be one of the following:

    importedKeyInitiallyDeferred
    importedKeyInitiallyImmediate
    importedKeyNotDeferrable.

String getDatabaseProductName( )
Returns the name of the database.

String getDatabaseProductVersion( )
Returns the version of the database.

int getDatabaseMajorVersion( )
    Returns the major version number of the database. (Java 1.4)

int getDatabaseMinorVersion( )
    Returns the minor version number of the database. (Java 1.4)

int getDefaultTransactionIsolation( )
    Returns the database's default transaction isolation level. It can be one of the following constants:

        TRANSACTION_NONE
        TRANSACTION_READ_COMMITTED
        TRANSACTION_READ_UNCOMMITTED
        TRANSACTION_REPEATABLE_READ
        TRANSACTION_SERIALIZABLE

int getDriverMajorVersion( )
    Returns the JDBC driver's major version number.

int getDriverMinorVersion( )
    Returns the JDBC driver's minor version number.

String getDriverName( )
    Returns the JDBC driver's name.

String getDriverVersion( )
    Returns the JDBC driver's version number.

ResultSet getExportedKeys(String catalog, String schema, String table)
    Returns a result set that describes the foreign key columns that reference the specified table's primary key. The result set is defined as follows:

    PKTABLE_CAT
        A String value of the primary key catalog name (may be null)

    PKTABLE_SCHEM
        A String value of the primary key schema name (may be null)

    PKTABLE_NAME
        A String value of the primary key table name

    PKCOLUMN_NAME
        A String value of a primary key column name

    FKTABLE_CAT
        A String value of the foreign key catalog name (may be null)

FKTABLE_SCHEM
> A String value of the foreign key schema name (may be null)

FKTABLE_NAME
> A String value of the foreign key table name

FKCOLUMN_NAME
> A String value of a foreign key column name

KEY_SEQ
> A short value indicating the sequence of a column within the foreign key

UPDATE_RULE
> A short value that describes what happens to the foreign key when the primary key is updated. It is one of the following constants:

```
    importedKeyNoAction
    importedKeyCascade
    importedKeySetNull
    importedKeySetDefault
    importedKeyRestrict
```

DELETE_RULE
> A short value that describes what happens to the foreign key when the primary key is deleted. It is one of the following constants:

```
    importedKeyNoAction
    importedKeyCascade
    importedKeySetNull
    importedKeySetDefault
    importedKeyRestrict
```

FK_NAME
> A String value of the foreign key name (may be null)

PK_NAME
> A String value of the primary key name (may be null)

DEFERRABILITY
> A short value that describes whether or not the evaluation of the foreign key constraints can be deferred until a transaction is committed. The value will match one of these constants:

```
    importedKeyInitiallyDeferred
    importedKeyInitiallyImmediate
    importedKeyNotDeferrable
```

`String getExtraNameCharacters( )`

Returns the nonalphanumeric characters that can be used in unquoted identifier names.

`String getIdentifierQuoteString( )`

Returns the string used to quote SQL identifiers.

`ResultSet getImportedKeys(String catalog, String schema, String table)`

Returns a result set that describes the primary key columns that reference the specified table's foreign keys. The result set is defined as follows:

PKTABLE_CAT

A `String` value of the primary key catalog name (may be null)

PKTABLE_SCHEM

A `String` value of the primary key schema name (may be null)

PKTABLE_NAME

A `String` value of the primary key table name

PKCOLUMN_NAME

A `String` value of the primary key column name

FKTABLE_CAT

A `String` value of the foreign key catalog name (may be null)

FKTABLE_SCHEM

A `String` value of the foreign key schema name (may be null)

FKTABLE_NAME

A `String` value of the foreign key table name

FKCOLUMN_NAME

A `String` value of a foreign key column name

KEY_SEQ

A `short` value indicating the sequence of a column within a foreign key

UPDATE_RULE

A `short` value that describes what happens to the foreign key when the primary key is updated. It is one of the following constants:

> importedKeyNoAction
> importedKeyCascade

> > importedKeySetNull
> > importedKeySetDefault
> > importedKeyRestrict

DELETE_RULE

> A short value that describes what happens to the foreign key when the primary key is deleted. It is one of the following constants:

> > importedKeyNoAction
> > importedKeyCascade
> > importedKeySetNull
> > importedKeySetDefault
> > importedKeyRestrict

FK_NAME

> A String value of a foreign key name (may be null)

PK_NAME

> A String value of a primary key name (may be null)

DEFERRABILITY

> A short value that describes whether the evaluation of the foreign key constraints can be deferred until the transaction is committed. It is one of the following constants:

> > importedKeyInitiallyDeferred
> > importedKeyInitiallyImmediate
> > importedKeyNotDeferrable

ResultSet getIndexInfo(String catalog, String schema,
  String table, boolean unique, boolean approximate)

> Returns a result set that describes a table's indices and statistics. The result set is defined as follows:

TABLE_CAT

> A String value of the table's catalog name (may be null)

TABLE_SCHEM

> A String value of the table's schema name (may be null)

TABLE_NAME

> A String value of the table's name

NON_UNIQUE

> A boolean value of true when the index's values can be non-unique

INDEX_QUALIFIER

> A String value of the index's catalog name (may be null)

INDEX_NAME

    A String value of an index's name

TYPE

    A short that describes the index type:

        tableIndexStatistic
        tableIndexClustered
        tableIndexHashed
        tableIndexOther

ORDINAL_POSITION

    A short value that describes the column sequence number within an index

COLUMN_NAME

    A String value of a column's name

ASC_OR_DESC

    A String value that describes the column sort sequence: "A" for ascending, "D" for descending (may be null)

CARDINALITY

    An int value that describes the number of rows in the table when INDEX_TYPE is tableIndexStatistic; otherwise, it's the number of unique values in the index

PAGES

    An int value that describes the number of pages used for the table when INDEX_TYPE is tableIndexStatisic; otherwise, it's the number of pages used for the current index

FILTER_CONDITION

    A String value for a filter condition, if one exists (may be null)

int getJDBCMajorVersion( )

Returns the major JDBC version number for this driver. (Java 1.4)

int getJDBCMinorVersion( )

Returns the minor JDBC version number for this driver. (Java 1.4)

int getMaxBinaryLiteralLength( )

Returns the number of possible hex characters in an inline binary literal.

int getMaxCatalogNameLength( )
> Returns the maximum length of a catalog name.

int getMaxCharLiteralLength( )
> Returns the maximum length for a character literal.

int getMaxColumnNameLength( )
> Returns the maximum length of a column name.

int getMaxColumnsInGroupBy( )
> Returns the maximum number of columns in a GROUP BY clause.

int getMaxColumnsInIndex( )
> Returns the maximum number of columns allowed in an index.

int getMaxColumnsInOrderBy( )
> Returns the maximum number of columns in an ORDER BY clause.

int getMaxColumnsInSelect( )
> Returns the maximum number of columns in a SELECT list.

int getMaxColumnsInTable( )
> Returns the maximum number of columns in a table.

int getMaxConnections( )
> Returns the maximum number of simultaneous connections that can exist for the database.

int getMaxCursorNameLength( )
> Returns the maximum cursor name length.

int getMaxIndexLength( )
> Returns the maximum size, in bytes, for an index, including all of the parts of the index.

int getMaxProcedureNameLength( )
> Returns the maximum length of a procedure name.

int getMaxRowSize( )
> Returns the maximum length of a single row.

int getMaxSchemaNameLength( )
> Returns the maximum length of a schema name.

int getMaxStatementLength( )
> Returns the maximum length of an SQL statement.

int getMaxStatements()

> Returns the maximum number of active statements that a user can have open to the database at one time.

int getMaxTableNameLength()

> Returns the maximum length of a table name.

int getMaxTablesInSelect()

> Returns the maximum number of tables that can be used in a SELECT statement.

int getMaxUserNameLength()

> Returns the maximum length of a username.

String getNumericFunctions()

> Returns a comma-separated list of all supported math functions.

ResultSet getPrimaryKeys(String catalog, String schema, String table)

> Returns a result set that describes a table's primary key columns. The result set is defined as follows:
>
> TABLE_CAT
>> A String value of the table's catalog name (may be null)
>
> TABLE_SCHEM
>> A String value of the table's schema name (may be null)
>
> TABLE_NAME
>> A String value of the table's name
>
> COLUMN_NAME
>> A String value of a primary key column's name
>
> KEY_SEQ
>> A short value indicating the sequence of the column in the primary key
>
> PK_NAME
>> A String value of the primary key name (may be null)

ResultSet getProcedureColumns(String catalog, String schemaPattern, String procedureNamePattern, String columnNamePattern)

> Returns a result set that describes stored procedure parameters and result columns. The result set is defined as follows:
>
> PROCEDURE_CAT
>> A String value of the procedure's catalog name (may be null; may be a package name for Oracle)

PROCEDURE_SCHEM
A String value of the procedure's schema name (may be null)

PROCEDURE_NAME
A String value of the procedure's name

COLUMN_NAME
A String value of the column/parameter name

COLUMN_TYPE
A short value that describes the kind of column/parameter. It is one of the following constants:

    procedureColumnUnknown
    procedureColumnIn
    procedureColumnInOut
    procedureColumnOut
    procedureColumnReturn
    procedureColumnResult

DATA_TYPE
A short value from java.sql.Types indicating the SQL type

TYPE_NAME
A String value of a database-dependent name or user-defined type (UDT) name

PRECISION
An int value that describes the precision of the data type

LENGTH
An int value that describes the length in bytes

SCALE
A short value that describes the scale of a numeric data type

RADIX
A short value that describes the radix of the data type

NULLABLE
A short value that describes the nullability of the column or parameter. It is one of the following constants:

    procedureNoNulls
    procedureNullable
    procedureNullableUnknown

REMARKS
A String value that is a comment describing the column/parameter

ResultSet getProcedures(String catalog, String schemaPattern,
    String procedureNamePattern)

Returns a result set that lists available stored procedures. The
result set is defined as follows:

PROCEDURE_CAT

A String value of a procedure's catalog name (may be
null; may be a package name for Oracle)

PROCEDURE_SCHEM

A String value of a procedure's schema name (may be
null)

PROCEDURE_NAME

A String value of a procedure's name

RESERVED_1

Reserved for future use

RESERVED_2

Reserved for future use

RESERVED_3

Reserved for future use

REMARKS

A String value that is an explanatory comment on the
procedure

PROCEDURE_TYPE

A short value that describes the kind of procedure. It is
one of the following constants:

    procedureResultUnknown
    procedureNoResult
    procedureReturnsResult

String getProcedureTerm()

Returns the database vendor's preferred term for "procedure."

int getResultSetHoldability()

Returns the default holdability of a ResultSet (Java 1.4):

    ResultSet.CLOSE_CURSORS_AT_COMMIT
    ResultSet.HOLD_CURSORS_OVER_COMMIT

ResultSet getSchemas()

Returns the list of names of this database's schemas.

TABLE_SCHEM

A String value of a table's schema name.

TABLE_CATALOG
> A String value of the catalog name (may be null). (Java 1. 4)

String getSchemaTerm( )
> Returns the database vendor's preferred term for "schema."

String getSearchStringEscape( )
> Returns this database's escape wildcard characters.

String getSQLKeywords( )
> Returns a comma-separated list of this database's non-SQL92 SQL keywords.

int getSQLStateType( )
> Returns one of the following constants that describe whether the SQLSTATE returned by SQLException's getSQLState( ) method is from X/Open SQL CLI or SQL:1999 (Java 1.4):

> sqlStateSQL99
> sqlStateXOpen

String getStringFunctions( )
> Returns a comma-separated list of this database's string functions.

ResultSet getSuperTables(String catalog, String schemaPattern, String tableNamePattern)
> Returns a result set that describes the table hierarchies defined in a particular schema. The result set is defined as follows:

TABLE_CAT
> A String value of a type's catalog name (may be null)

TABLE_SCHEM
> A String value of a type's schema name (may be null)

TABLE_NAME
> A String value of a type's name

SUPERTABLE_NAME
> A String value of a direct super type name (Java 1.4)

ResultSet getSuperTypes(String catalog, String schemaPattern, String typeNamePattern)
> Returns a result set that describes user-defined type (UDT) hierarchies defined in a particular schema. The result set is defined as follows:

TYPE_CAT
> A String value of the UDT's catalog name (may be null)

TYPE_SCHEM

A String value of the UDT's schema name (may be null)

TYPE_NAME

A String value of the UDT's type name

SUPERTYPE_CAT

A String value of the direct super type's catalog name (may be null)

SUPERTYPE_SCHEM

A String value of the direct super type's schema name (may be null)

SUPERTYPE_NAME

A String value of the direct super type's name (Java 1.4)

String getSystemFunctions()

Returns a comma-separated list of the database's system functions.

ResultSet getTablePrivileges(String catalog,
  String schemaPattern, String tableNamePattern)

Returns a result set that describes the access rights for each table available in a catalog. The result set is defined as follows:

TABLE_CAT

A String value of the table's catalog name (may be null)

TABLE_SCHEM

A String value of the table's schema name (may be null)

TABLE_NAME

A String value of the table's name

GRANTOR

A String value indicating the grantor of access (may be null)

GRANTEE

A String value indicating the grantee of access

PRIVILEGE

A String value with the name of an access privilege (SELECT, INSERT, UPDATE, REFRENCES, etc.)

IS_GRANTABLE

A String value that describes whether the privilege is grantable by the grantee. It is YES if grantable, otherwise NO, or null if the grantability is unknown.

ResultSet getTables(String catalog, String schemaPattern,
    String tableNamePattern, String[ ] types)

Returns a result set that lists the tables available in a catalog.
The result set is defined as follows:

TABLE_CAT

A String value of the table's catalog name (may be null)

TABLE_SCHEM

A String value of the table's schema name (may be null)

TABLE_NAME

A String value of the table's name

TABLE_TYPE

A String value indicating the table's type, which will be
one of the following values: TABLE, VIEW, SYSTEM TABLE,
GLOBAL TEMPORARY, LOCAL TEMPORARY, ALIAS, or SYNONYM

REMARKS

A String value that is an explanatory comment on the
table

TYPE_CAT

A String value of the type's catalog (may be null)

TYPE_SCHEM

A String value of the type's schema (may be null)

TYPE_NAME

A String value of the type's name (may be null)

SELF_REFERENCING_COL_NAME

A String value of the name of the designated "identifier"
column (may be null)

REF_GENERATION

A String value that specifies how values in SELF_
REFERENCING_COL_NAME are created. Possible
values are SYSTEM, USER, and DERIVED (may be null)

ResultSet getTableTypes( )

Returns a result set that lists the table types available in this
database. The result set is defined as follows:

TABLE_TYPE

A String value of one or more of the following table type
literals: TABLE, VIEW, SYSTEM TABLE, GLOBAL TEMPORARY,
LOCAL TEMPORARY, ALIAS, or SYNONYM

String getTimeDateFunctions( )

    Returns a comma-separated list of date and time functions.

ResultSet getTypeInfo( )

    Returns a result set that describes all the standard SQL types supported by this database. The result set is defined as follows:

TYPE_NAME

    A String value of a type's name

DATA_TYPE

    A short value from java.sql.Types indicating the SQL data type

PRECISION

    An int value that describes the maximum size or precision for a numeric type

LITERAL_PREFIX

    A String value that is the prefix used to quote a literal (may be null)

LITERAL_SUFFIX

    A String value that is the suffix used to quote a literal (may be null)

CREATE_PARAMS

    A String value that describes the parameters used in creating the type (may be null)

NULLABLE

    A short value that describes whether you can use an SQL NULL for this type. It is one of the following constants:

        typeNoNulls
        typeNullable
        typeNullableUnknown

CASE_SENSITIVE

    A boolean value of true if the type is case-sensitive

SEARCHABLE

    A short value that describes whether you can use this type in a WHERE clause. It is one of the following constants:

        typePredNone
        typePredChar
        typePredBasic
        typeSearchable

UNSIGNED_ATTRIBUTE
> A boolean value of true if the type is unsigned

FIXED_PREC_SCALE
> A boolean value of true if the type can be used as a money value

AUTO_INCREMENT
> A boolean value of true if the type can be used as an auto-increment value

LOCAL_TYPE_NAME
> A String value that names a localized version of the name (may be null)

MINIMUM_SCALE
> A short value of the minimum scale supported

MAXIMUM_SCALE
> A short value of the maximum scale supported

SQL_DATA_TYPE
> An int that is an unused value

SQL_DATETIME_SUB
> An int that is an unused value

NUM_PREC_RADIX
> An int value that describes the radix of the type (usually 2 or 10)

ResultSet getUDTs(String catalog, String schemaPattern, String typeNamePattern, int[ ] types)
> Returns a result set that describes the user-defined types (UDTs) defined in a particular schema. The result set is defined as follows:

TYPE_CAT
> A String value of a type's catalog name (may be null)

TYPE_SCHEM
> A String value of a type's schema name (may be null)

TYPE_NAME
> A String value of a type's name

CLASS_NAME
> A String value of the type's Java class name associated by the current connection's type map

---

DATA_TYPE

> A String value of the type as defined in java.sql.Types, which will be one of the following literals: JAVA_OBJECT, STRUCT, or DISTINCT

REMARKS

> A String value that is an explanatory comment on the type (Java 1.2)

BASE_TYPE

> A short value from java.sql.Types that is the type code of the source type of a DISTINCT type, or the type that implements the user-generated reference type of the SELF_REFERENCING_COLUMN of a structured type (null if DATA_TYPE is not DISTINCT, or if it's not a STRUCT with REFERENCE_GENERATION = USER_DEFINED)

String getURL( )

> Returns the URL for this database.

String getUserName( )

> Returns the current username.

ResultSet getVersionColumns(String catalog, String schema, String table)

> Returns a result set that lists any columns that are automatically updated when any value in a row is updated. The result set is defined as follows:

SCOPE

> A short value that is not used

COLUMN_NAME

> A String value of the column's name

DATA_TYPE

> A short value of the SQL data type from java.sql.Types

TYPE_NAME

> A String value of the data source–dependent type name

COLUMN_SIZE

> An int value that is the column's length, or its precision if the data type is numeric

BUFFER_LENGTH

> An int value representing the length of the column value in bytes

DECIMAL_DIGITS
> A short value of the scale if the data type is numeric

PSEUDO_COLUMN
> A short value that describes whether the column is a pseudo column. It is one of the following constants:
>
> > versionColumnUnknown
> > versionColumnNotPseudo
> > versionColumnPseudo

boolean locatorsUpdateCopy( )
> Returns true if updates made to a LOB are made on a copy, or false if they are made directly to the LOB. (Java 1.4)

boolean insertsAreDetected(int resultSetType)
> Returns true if a visible row insert can be detected by calling ResultSet.rowInserted( ). (Java 1.2)

boolean isCatalogAtStart( )
> Returns true if a catalog appears at the start of a qualified table name.

boolean isReadOnly( )
> Returns true if the database is in read-only mode.

boolean nullPlusNonNullIsNull( )
> Returns true if a concatenation between NULL and a non-NULL value is NULL.

boolean nullsAreSortedAtEnd( )
> Returns true if NULL values are sorted to the end of a list regardless of sort order.

boolean nullsAreSortedAtStart( )
> Returns true if NULL values are sorted to the start of a list regardless of sort order.

boolean nullsAreSortedHigh( )
> Returns true if NULL values are sorted high.

boolean nullsAreSortedLow( )
> Returns true if NULL values are sorted low.

boolean othersDeletesAreVisible(int resultSettype)
> Returns true if deletes made by others are visible. (Java 1.2)

boolean othersInsertsAreVisible(int resultSettype)
> Returns true if inserts made by others are visible. (Java 1.2)

boolean othersUpdatesAreVisible(int resultSettype)
> Returns true if updates made by others are visible. (Java 1.2)

---

boolean ownDeletesAreVisible(int resultSettype)
>   Returns true if a result set's own deletes are visible. (Java 1.2)

boolean ownInsertsAreVisible(int resultSettype)
>   Returns true if a result set's own inserts are visible. (Java 1.2)

boolean ownUpdatesAreVisible(int resultSettype)
>   Returns true if a result set's own updates are visible. (Java 1.2)

boolean storesLowerCaseIdentifiers( )
>   Returns true if the database treats mixed-case unquoted SQL identifiers as case-insensitive and stores them as lowercase.

boolean storesLowerCaseQuotedIdentifiers( )
>   Returns true if the database treats mixed-case quoted SQL identifiers as case-insensitive and stores them as lowercase.

boolean storesMixedCaseIdentifiers( )
>   Returns true if the database treats mixed-case unquoted SQL identifiers as case-insensitive and stores them as mixed case.

boolean storesMixedCaseQuotedIdentifiers( )
>   Returns true if the database treats mixed-case quoted SQL identifiers as case-insensitive and stores them as mixed case.

boolean storesUpperCaseIdentifiers( )
>   Returns true if the database treats mixed-case unquoted SQL identifiers as case-insensitive and stores them as uppercase.

boolean storesUpperCaseQuotedIdentifiers( )
>   Returns true if the database treats mixed-case quoted SQL identifiers as case-insensitive and stores them as uppercase.

boolean supportsAlterTableWithAddColumn( )
>   Returns true if the database supports adding a column with ALTER TABLE.

boolean supportsAlterTableWithDropColumn( )
>   Returns true if the database supports dropping a column with ALTER TABLE.

boolean supportsANSI92EntryLevelSQL( )
>   Returns true if the driver and database support ANSI92 entry-level SQL grammar.

boolean supportsANSI92FullSQL( )
>   Returns true if the driver and database support ANSI92 full SQL grammar.

`boolean supportsANSI92IntermediateSQL( )`
Returns true if the driver and database support ANSI92 intermediate SQL grammar.

`boolean supportsBatchUpdates( )`
Returns true if the driver supports batch updates. (Java 1.2)

`boolean supportsCatalogsInDataManipulation( )`
Returns true if a catalog name can be used in a data manipulation statement.

`boolean supportsCatalogsInIndexDefinitions( )`
Returns true if a catalog name can be used in an index definition statement.

`boolean supportsCatalogsInPrivilegeDefinitions( )`
Returns true if a catalog name can be used in a privilege definition statement.

`boolean supportsCatalogsInProcedureCalls( )`
Returns true if a catalog name can be used in a procedure call statement.

`boolean supportsCatalogsInTableDefinitions( )`
Returns true if a catalog name can be used in a table definition statement.

`boolean supportsColumnAliasing( )`
Returns true if column aliasing is supported.

`boolean supportsConvert( )`
Returns true if the CONVERT function between SQL types is supported.

`boolean supportsConvert(int fromType, int toType)`
Returns true if the CONVERT function between the given SQL types is supported.

`boolean supportsCoreSQLGrammar( )`
Returns true if ODBC core SQL grammar is supported.

`boolean supportsCorrelatedSubqueries( )`
Returns true if correlated subqueries are supported

`boolean supportsDataDefinitionAndDataManipulationTransactions( )`
Returns true if both DDL and DML statements within a transaction are supported.

`boolean supportsDataManipulationTransactionsOnly( )`
Returns true if only DML statements within a transaction are supported.

boolean supportsDifferentTableCorrelationNames( )
>   Returns true if table correlation names are supported and are
>   required to be different from the names of the tables.

boolean supportsExpressionsInOrderBy( )
>   Returns true if expressions in an ORDER BY list are
>   supported.

boolean supportsExtendedSQLGrammar( )
>   Returns true if ODBC extended SQL grammar is supported.

boolean supportsFullOuterJoins( )
>   Returns true if full nested outer joins are supported.

boolean supportsGetGeneratedKeys( )
>   Returns true if autogenerated keys can be retrieved after a
>   statement has been executed. (Java 1.4)

boolean supportsGroupBy( )
>   Returns true if some form of a GROUP BY clause is
>   supported.

boolean supportsGroupByBeyondSelect( )
>   Returns true if a GROUP BY clause can add columns not in
>   the SELECT statement.

boolean supportsGroupByUnrelated( )
>   Returns true if a GROUP BY clause can use columns not in a
>   SELECT statement.

boolean supportsIntegrityEnhancementFacility( )
>   Returns true if SQL integrity constraints are supported.

boolean supportsLikeEscapeClause( )
>   Returns true if the escape character is supported in LIKE
>   clauses.

boolean supportsLimitedOuterJoins( )
>   Returns true if there is limited support for outer joins.

boolean supportsMinimumSQLGrammar( )
>   Returns true if ODBC minimum SQL grammar is supported.

boolean supportsMixedCaseIdentifiers( )
>   Returns true if the database treats mixed-case, unquoted SQL
>   identifiers as case-sensitive and stores them as mixed case.

boolean supportsMixedCaseQuotedIdentifiers( )
>   Returns true if the database treats mixed-case, quoted SQL
>   identifiers as case-sensitive and stores them as mixed case.

`boolean supportsMultipleOpenResults( )`

Returns true if it is possible to have multiple result sets returned from a callable statement. (Java 1.4)

`boolean supportsMultipleResultSets( )`

Returns true if multiple result sets from a single execute are supported.

`boolean supportsMultipleTransactions( )`

Returns true if you can have multiple transactions open simultaneously.

`boolean supportsNamedParameters( )`

Returns true if the database supports named parameters to callable statements. (Java 1.4)

`boolean supportsNonNullableColumns( )`

Returns true if columns can be defined as non-nullable.

`boolean supportsOpenCursorsAcrossCommit( )`

Returns true if cursors remain open across commits.

`boolean supportsOpenCursorsAcrossRollback( )`

Returns true if cursors remain open across rollbacks.

`boolean supportsOpenStatementsAcrossCommit( )`

Returns true if statements remain open across commits.

`boolean supportsOpenStatementsAcrossRollback( )`

Returns true if statements remain open across rollbacks.

`boolean supportsOrderByUnrelated( )`

Returns true if an ORDER BY clause can use columns not in the SELECT statement.

`boolean supportsOuterJoins( )`

Returns true if some form of outer join is supported.

`boolean supportsPositionedDelete( )`

Returns true if a positioned DELETE is supported.

`boolean supportsPositionedUpdate( )`

Returns true if a positioned UPDATE is supported.

`boolean supportsResultSetConcurrency(int resultSettype,`
`  int resultSetConcurrency)`

Returns true if the database supports the concurrency type in combination with the given result set type. (Java 1.2)

`boolean supportsResultSetHoldability(int holdability)`

Returns true if the database supports the specified result set holdability. (Java 1.4)

```
boolean supportsResultSetType(int resultSettype)
```
Returns true if the database supports the given result set type. (Java 1.2)

```
boolean supportsSavepoints()
```
Returns true if the database supports savepoints. (Java 1.4)

```
boolean supportsSchemasInDataManipulation()
```
Returns true if a schema name can be used in a data manipulation statement.

```
boolean supportsSchemasInIndexDefinitions()
```
Returns true if a schema name can be used in an index definition statement.

```
boolean supportsSchemasInPrivilegeDefinitions()
```
Returns true if a schema name can be used in a privilege definition statement.

```
boolean supportsSchemasInProcedureCalls()
```
Returns true if a schema name can be used in a procedure call statement.

```
boolean supportsSchemasInTableDefinitions()
```
Returns true if a schema name can be used in a table definition statement.

```
boolean supportsSelectForUpdate()
```
Returns true if SELECT FOR UPDATE is supported.

```
boolean supportsStatementPooling()
```
Returns true if the database supports statement pooling. (Java 1.4)

```
boolean supportsStoredProcedures()
```
Returns true if stored procedure calls using JDBC escape syntax are supported.

```
boolean supportsSubqueriesInComparisons()
```
Returns true if subqueries in comparison expressions are supported.

```
boolean supportsSubqueriesInExists()
```
Returns true if subqueries in EXISTS expressions are supported.

```
boolean supportsSubqueriesInIns()
```
Returns true if subqueries in IN expressions are supported.

```
boolean supportsSubqueriesInQuantifieds()
```
Returns true if subqueries in quantified expressions are supported.

```
boolean supportsTableCorrelationNames()
```
Returns true if table correlation names are supported.

```
boolean supportsTransactionIsolationLevel(
   int transactionLevel)
```
Returns true if a database supports the given transaction isolation level.

```
boolean supportsTransactions()
```
Returns true if transactions are supported.

```
boolean supportsUnion()
```
Returns true if the SQL keyword UNION is supported.

```
boolean supportsUnionAll()
```
Returns true if the SQL keyword UNION ALL is supported.

```
boolean updatesAreDetected(int resultSettype)
```
Returns true if a visible row update can be detected by calling the method ResultSet.rowUpdated(). (Java 1.2)

```
boolean usesLocalFilePerTable()
```
Returns true if the database uses a file for each table.

```
boolean usesLocalFiles()
```
Returns true if the database stores tables in a local file.

DataSource   Java 1.4, JDBC 2.0 OP

Interface name: javax.sql.DataSource

DataSource is a factory for database connections. A data source is typically retrieved via JNDI. All of its methods can throw an SQLException.

Methods

```
Connection getConnection()
```
Returns a new database connection using the connection properties specified when the data source was stored in a JNDI directory, or by using the JDBC driver vendor's proprietary methods.

Connection getConnection(String username, String password)
    Returns a new database connection using the specified username and password along with any connection properties specified when the data source was stored in a JNDI directory, or by using the JDBC driver vendor's proprietary methods.

int getLoginTimeout( )
    Returns the maximum amount of time the data source will wait while attempting to establish a connection, in seconds.

PrintWriter getLogWriter( )
    Returns the log writer for the data source.

void setLoginTimeout(int seconds)
    Sets the maximum amount of time the data source will wait while attempting to establish a connection, in seconds.

void setLogWriter(PrintWriter out)
    Sets the log writer for the data source.

DataTruncation

Class name: java.sql.DataTruncation	Extends java.sql.SQLWarning Implements java.io.Serializable

DataTruncation is an exception used when the JDBC driver truncates data. It is used as a warning on reads, or as an exception on writes. The SQLState value is 01004.

Constructor

DataTruncation(int index, boolean parameter, boolean read,
    int dataSize, int transferSize)

Methods

int getDataSize( )
    Returns the number of bytes that should have been read or written, or -1 if that value is unknown.

int getIndex( )
    Returns the parameter index of the truncated parameter or column.

boolean getParameter( )
    Returns true if a parameter value was truncated, false if a column value was truncated.

boolean getRead( )
    Returns true if the value was truncated on a read, false if
    truncated on a write.

getTransferSize( )
    Returns the number of bytes that were actually read or
    written, or -1 if that value is unknown.

Methods inherited from java.sql.SQLWarning

SQLWarning getNextWarning( )
void setNextWarning(SQLWarning w)

Methods inherited from java.sql.SQLException

int getErrorCode( )
SQLException getNextException( )
String getSQLState( )
void setNextException(SQLException ex)

Date

Class name: java.sql.Date   Extends java.util.Date
                           Implements Cloneable, Comparable, Serializable

Date is a wrapper class that allows JDBC to identify a date as an
SQL DATE.

Constructor

Date(long date)

Methods

void setTime(long milliseconds)
    Sets the date to the given millisecond value.

String toString( )
    Formats the date in the JDBC date escape format: yyyy-mm-dd.

static Date valueOf(String s)
    Parses a string in JDBC date escape format to a Date value.

Methods inherited from java.util.Date

boolean after(Date when)
boolean before(Date when)
Object clone( )
int compareTo(Date anotherDate)

```
int compareTo(Object o)
boolean equals(Object obj)
long getTime( )
int hashCode( )
```

Driver

Interface name: java.sql.Driver

Driver is the JDBC driver interface that must be implemented by every JDBC driver.

Methods

boolean acceptsURL(String url) throws SQLException
> Returns true if the driver determines that it can open a connection to the given URL.

Connection connect(String url, Properties info)
  throws SQLException
> Tries to establish a connection to a database using the given URL.

int getMajorVersion( )
> Returns the driver's major version number.

int getMinorVersion( )
> Returns the driver's minor version number.

DriverPropertyInfo[ ] getPropertyInfo(String url,
  Properties info) throws SQLException
> Returns a list of possible properties for the driver.

boolean jdbcCompliant( )
> Returns true if this driver is a JDBC-compliant driver.

DriverManager

Class name: java.sql.DriverManager   Extends java.lang.Object

DriverManager is a utility class used to manage JDBC drivers and, accordingly, establish connections to a database (the DataSource interface can also be used to establish connections to a database). JDBC drivers can be loaded at any time by using:

```
Class.forName("driverClassName");
```

When one of its getConnection( ) methods is called, DriverManager attempts to locate a suitable driver from all those loaded. If it finds a suitable driver, it attempts to establish a connection using that driver.

Methods

```
static void deregisterDriver(Driver driver)
  throws SQLException
```
Removes a JDBC driver from driver manager's list.

```
static Connection getConnection(String url)
  throws SQLException
```
Attempts to establish a connection to a database using only information in the specified URL.

```
static Connection getConnection(String url, Properties info)
  throws SQLException
```
Attempts to establish a connection to a database using information in the specified URL and `Properties` object.

```
static Connection getConnection(String url, String user,
  String password) throws SQLException
```
Attempts to establish a connection to a database using information in the specified URL, user, and password.

```
static Driver getDriver(String url) throws SQLException
```
Attempts to locate a driver that understands the specified URL.

```
static Enumeration getDrivers( )
```
Returns an enumeration of all currently loaded JDBC drivers.

```
static int getLoginTimeout( )
```
Returns the maximum time that the driver can wait when attempting to log in to a database, in seconds.

```
static PrintWriter getLogWriter( )
```
Returns the current log writer. (Java 1.2)

```
static void println(String message)
```
Prints a message to the log.

```
static void registerDriver(Driver driver) throws SQLException
```
Registers the specified driver.

```
static void setLoginTimeout(int seconds)
```
Sets the maximum time that a driver will wait while attempting to connect to a database, in seconds.

```
static void setLogWriter(PrintWriter out)
```
Sets the `PrintWriter` object that is used by `DriverManager`, and any subsequently used drivers, for logging. (Java 1.2)

DriverPropertyInfo

Class name: java.sql.DriverPropertyInfo   Extends java.lang.Object

DriverPropertyInfo is a class used to describe JDBC driver properties.

Constructor

DriverPropertyInfo(String name, String value)

Fields

String[ ] choices
    An array of possible choices for a property value

String description
    A property's description

String name
    A property's name

boolean required
    true if this is a property that is required to establish a connection using Driver.connect( )

String value
    The current value of a property

Object

Class name: java.lang.Object

Object is the root of the Java class hierarchy; therefore, all objects implement its methods.

Constructor

Object( )

Methods

protected Object clone( )
  throws CloneNotSupportedException, OutOfMemoryError
    Returns a clone of the object.

boolean equals(Object obj)
    Returns true if obj is considered to be equal to this object, otherwise false.

protected void finalize( ) throws Throwable
  Called just before this object is garbage-collected.

Class getClass( )
  Returns the runtime Class of this object.

int hashCode( )
  Returns the hash code for this object.

void notify( ) throws IllegalMonitorStateException
  Notifies a single thread waiting on this object's monitor to wake up.

void notifyAll( ) throws IllegalMonitorStateException
  Notifies all threads waiting on this object's monitor to wake up.

String toString( )
  Returns a string representation of this object.

void wait( )
  throws IllegalMonitorStateException, InterruptedException
  Puts this object's thread into a wait state until another thread invokes this object's notify( ) or notifyAll( ) method.

void wait(long timeout) throws IllegalArgumentException,
  IllegalMonitorStateException, InterruptedException
  Puts this object's thread into a wait state until another thread invokes this object's notify( ) or notifyAll( ) method, or for timeout milliseconds.

void wait(long timeout, int nanos)
  throws IllegalArgumentException,
  IllegalMonitorStateException, InterruptedException
  Puts this object's thread into a wait state until another thread invokes this object's notify( ) or notifyAll( ) method, or for (timeout × 1,000,000) + nanos nanoseconds.

ParameterMetaData   Java 1.4

Interface name: java.sql.ParameterMetaData

ParameterMetaData is used to describe the parameters in a prepared statement. All of its methods can throw an SQLException.

Fields

static int parameterModeIn
  An IN parameter

static int parameterModeInOut
    An IN OUT parameter

static int parameterModeOut
    An OUT parameter

static int parameterModeUnknown
    The mode of the parameter is unknown

static int parameterNoNulls
    The parameter is not nullable

static int parameterNullable
    The parameter is nullable

static int parameterNullableUnknown
    The nullability of the parameter is unknown

Methods

String getParameterClassName(int parameterIndex)
    Returns the specified parameter's fully qualified Java class
    name to be used with PreparedStatement's setObject()
    method.

int getParameterCount()
    Returns the number of parameters in the prepared statement.

int getParameterMode(int parameterIndex)
    Returns the specified parameter's mode. It is one of the
    following constants:

        parameterModeIn
        parameterModeInOut
        parameterModeOut

int getParameterType(int parameterIndex)
    Returns the specified parameter's java.sql.Types constant.

String getParameterTypeName(int parameterIndex)
    Returns the specified parameter's database-specific type
    name.

int getPrecision(int parameterIndex)
    Returns the specified parameter's number of decimal digits.

int getScale(int parameterIndex)
    Returns the number of digits the specified parameter supports
    to the right of the decimal point.

int isNullable(int parameterIndex)
> Returns the specified parameter's nullability. It is one of the following constants:

>> parameterNoNulls
>> parameterNullable
>> parameterNullableUnknown

boolean isSigned(int parameterIndex)
> Returns true if the specified parameter can be a signed number.

PooledConnection

Java 1.4, JDBC 2.0 OP

Interface name: javax.sql.PooledConnection   Subinterfaces: javax.sql.XAConnection

PooledConnection is a wrapper for a DataSource that provides hooks for connection pool management. (Java 1.4, JDBC 2.0 OP)

Methods

void addConnectionEventListener(
  ConnectionEventListener listener)
> Adds a connection event listener.

void close( ) throws SQLException
> Closes the physical connection to a database.

Connection getConnection( ) throws SQLException
> Returns a physical connection to a database.

void removeConnectionEventListener(
  ConnectionEventListener listener)
> Removes a connection event listener.

PreparedStatement

Interface name: java.sql.PreparedStatement   Extends java.sql.Statement
                                    Subinterfaces: java.sql.CallableStatement

PreparedStatement is a class used to precompile and execute SQL statements. All of its methods can throw an SQLException.

Methods

void addBatch( )
> Adds the current SQL statement to this prepared statement's batch. (Java 1.2)

void clearParameters( )

Clears the current SQL statement's parameter values.

boolean execute( )

Executes the current precompiled SQL statement. It returns true if the SQL statement creates a result set, otherwise false.

ResultSet executeQuery( )

Executes the current precompiled SELECT statement returning its result set.

int executeUpdate( )

Executes the current precompiled INSERT, UPDATE, or DELETE statement, returning the number of rows affected.

ResultSetMetaData getMetaData( )

Returns the result set metadata for the current precompiled SELECT statement. (Java 1.2)

ParameterMetaData getParameterMetaData( )

Returns a parameter metadata object that describes this prepared statement's parameters. (Java 1.4)

NOTE

All of the following mutator or setXXX( ) methods set the specified SQL IN parameter value for the specified parameter index (starting from 1, incrementing left to right) in the SQL statement.

---

void setArray(int parameterIndex, Array x)

Sets a value using the specified Array. (Java 1.2)

void setAsciiStream(int parameterIndex, InputStream x, int length)

Sets a value using the first length bytes of the specified input stream.

void setBigDecimal(int parameterIndex, BigDecimal x)

Sets a value using the specified java.math.BigDecimal.

void setBinaryStream(int parameterIndex, InputStream x, int length)

Sets a value using the first length bytes of the specified input stream.

void setBlob(int parameterIndex, Blob x)
>   Sets a BLOB locator, not the BLOB value. Use Blob's setBinaryStream( ) to set the BLOB value. (Java 1.2)

void setBoolean(int parameterIndex, boolean x)
>   Sets a value using the specified boolean.

void setByte(int parameterIndex, byte x)
>   Sets a value using the specified byte.

void setBytes(int parameterIndex, byte[ ] x)
>   Sets a value using the specified byte array.

void setCharacterStream(int parameterIndex, Reader reader, int length)
>   Sets a value using the first length characters of the specified reader. (Java 1.2)

void setClob(int parameterIndex, Clob x)
>   Sets a CLOB locator, not the CLOB value. Use Clob's setCharacterStream( ) to set the CLOB value. (Java 1.2)

void setDate(int parameterIndex, Date x)
>   Sets a value using the specified java.sql.Date.

void setDate(int parameterIndex, Date x, Calendar calendar)
>   Sets a value using the specified java.sql.Date and Calendar. (Java 1.2)

void setDouble(int parameterIndex, double x)
>   Sets a value using the specified double.

void setFloat(int parameterIndex, float x)
>   Sets a value using the specified float.

void setInt(int parameterIndex, int x)
>   Sets a value using the specified int.

void setLong(int parameterIndex, long x)
>   Sets a value using the specified long.

void setNull(int parameterIndex, int sqlType)
>   Sets the specified parameter to an SQL NULL value. Pass a java.sql.Types constant to specify the parameter's type.

void setNull(int parameterIndex, int sqlType, String typeName)
>   Sets the specified parameter to an SQL NULL value for the specified user-defined type (UDT). (Java 1.2)

void setObject(int parameterIndex, Object x)
>   Sets the value using the specified Object.

void setObject(int parameterIndex, Object x, int sqlType)
    Sets a value using the specified Object and java.sql.Types constant.

void setObject(int parameterIndex, Object x, int sqlType,
  int scale)
    Sets a value using the specified Object, java.sql.Types constant, and scale (for numeric data types).

void setRef(int parameterIndex, Ref x)
    Sets a value using the specified Ref. (Java 1.2)

void setShort(int parameterIndex, short x)
    Sets a value using the specified short.

void setString(int parameterIndex, String x)
    Sets a value using the specified String.

void setTime(int parameterIndex, Time x)
    Sets a value using the specified Time.

void setTime(int parameterIndex, Time x,
  Calendar calendar)
    Sets a value using the specified Time and Calendar. (Java 1.2)

void setTimestamp(int parameterIndex, Timestamp x)
    Sets a value using the specified Timestamp.

void setTimestamp(int parameterIndex, Timestamp x,
  Calendar calendar)
    Sets a value using the specified Timestamp and Calendar. (Java 1.2)

void setURL(int parameterIndex, URL x)
    Sets a value using the specified java.net.URL. (Java 1.4)

Methods inherited from java.sql.Statement

```
void addBatch(String sql)
void cancel( )
void clearBatch( )
void clearWarnings( )
void close( )
boolean execute(String sql)
boolean execute(String sql, int autoGeneratedKeys)
boolean execute(String sql, int[ ] columnIndexes)
boolean execute(String sql, String[ ] columnNames)
int[ ] executeBatch( )
ResultSet executeQuery(String sql)
int executeUpdate(String sql)
```

```
int executeUpdate(String sql, int autoGeneratedKeys)
int executeUpdate(String sql, int[ ] columnIndexes)
int executeUpdate(String sql, String[ ] columnNames)
Connection getConnection( )
int getFetchDirection( )
int getFetchSize( )
ResultSet getGeneratedKeys( )
int getMaxFieldSize( )
int getMaxRows( )
boolean getMoreResults( )
boolean getMoreResults(int current)
int getQueryTimeout( )
ResultSet getResultSet( )
int getResultSetConcurrency( )
int getResultSetHoldability( )
int getResultSetType( )
int getUpdateCount( )
SQLWarning getWarnings( )
void setCursorName(String name)
void setEscapeProcessing(boolean enable)
void setFetchDirection(int direction)
void setFetchSize(int rows)
void setMaxFieldSize(int max)
void setMaxRows(int max)
void setQueryTimeout(int seconds)
```

Ref

Java 1.2

Interface name: java.sql.Ref

Ref represents an instance of the SQL type REF, which in turn is a reference to a structured type or user-defined type (UDT). All of its methods can throw an SQLException.

Methods

String getBaseTypeName( )
> Returns the database-specific type name, or UDT SQL type name, for the object of this Ref.

Object getObject( )
> Returns the UDT instance referenced by this Ref object using the current type map. (Java 1.4)

Object getObject(Map map)
> Returns the UDT instance referenced by this Ref object using the specified type map. (Java 1.4)

```
void setObject(Object value)
```
Sets the UDT that this Ref object references to the specified Object. (Java 1.4)

ResultSet

Interface name: java.sql.ResultSet

ResultSet is an abstract representation of a result set from a relational database query. Accordingly, each row in a ResultSet represents a row from the query, and each column in a ResultSet represents a column in the query. A ResultSet's cursor initially points before the first row.

The accessor, or getXXX(), methods and the mutator, or updateXXX(), methods have an index parameter that points to the column in the SQL query that is being accessed. Columns are numbered starting from 1, incrementing from left to right. When using the getXXX() methods, you can use wasNull() to determine if the last use of getXXX() returned a database NULL value. In addition, if you need to access the data from a particular column more than once while positioned on a row, it is advisable to store the value in a variable, because some JDBC drivers return garbage values or generate an SQL exception on the second access to a column.

Although Sun's JDBC documentation states that a ResultSet is automatically closed when the Statement, PreparedStatement, or CallableStatement that created it is closed, some JDBC drivers do not adhere to this rule, so it is advisable to manually close a ResultSet. All of ResultSet's methods can throw an SQLException.

Fields

```
static int CLOSE_CURSORS_AT_COMMIT
```
Close result set objects when the Connection's commit() method is called.

```
static int CONCUR_READ_ONLY
```
This result set can only be read.

```
static int CONCUR_UPDATABLE
```
This result set can be read and updated.

static int FETCH_FORWARD
> This result set's rows will be read in a forward direction, first-to-last, when calling next( ).

static int FETCH_REVERSE
> This result set's rows will be read in a reverse direction, last-to-first, when calling next( ).

static int FETCH_UNKNOWN
> This result set's fetch direction is unknown.

static int HOLD_CURSORS_OVER_COMMIT
> Do not close result set objects when the Connection's commit( ) method is called.

static int TYPE_FORWARD_ONLY
> This result set's cursor can only move forward.

static int TYPE_SCROLL_INSENSITIVE
> This result set's cursor is scrollable, but it does not detect changes made to its underlying database data by other users.

static int TYPE_SCROLL_SENSITIVE
> This result set's cursor is scrollable, and it does, at some level, detect changes made to its underlying database data by other users.

Methods

boolean absolute(int row)
> Moves the cursor to the specified row. (Java 1.2)

void afterLast( )
> Moves the cursor to just after the last row. (Java 1.2)

void beforeFirst( )
> Moves the cursor to just before the first row. (Java 1.2)

void cancelRowUpdates( )
> Cancels updates made to the current row. (Java 1.2)

void clearWarnings( )
> Clears any SQL warnings.

void close( )
> Closes this result set.

void deleteRow( )
> Deletes the current row. (Java 1.2)

int findColumn(String columnName)
> Returns the column index number for the specified column name.

boolean first()
> Moves the cursor to the first row. (Java 1.2)

NOTE

The following getXXX() methods that have a columnIndex or columnName parameter all get a result set's column value for the specified column index (starting from 1, incrementing from left to right), or column name, and map the database's value to the return data type.

Array getArray(int columnIndex)
Array getArray(String columnName)
> Returns a value as an Array. (Java 1.2)

InputStream getAsciiStream(int columnIndex)
InputStream getAsciiStream(String columnName)
> Returns an InputStream to be used to retrieve the database value as an ASCII stream.

BigDecimal getBigDecimal(int columnIndex)
BigDecimal getBigDecimal(String columnName)
> Returns the value as a java.math.BigDecimal. (Java 1.2)

InputStream getBinaryStream(int columnIndex)
InputStream getBinaryStream(String columnName)
> Returns an InputStream to be used to retrieve the database value as a binary stream.

Blob getBlob(int columnIndex)
Blob getBlob(String columnName)
> Returns a Blob locator, not the BLOB value. Use the Blob's getBinaryStream() to retrieve the BLOB value using an InputStream. (Java 1.2)

boolean getBoolean(int columnIndex)
boolean getBoolean(String columnName)
> Returns a value as a boolean.

byte getByte(int columnIndex)
byte getByte(String columnName)
> Returns a value as a byte.

```
byte[ ] getBytes(int columnIndex)
byte[ ] getBytes(String columnName)
```
Returns a value as a byte array.

```
Reader getCharacterStream(int columnIndex)
Reader getCharacterStream(String columnName)
```
Returns a Reader that will be used to retrieve the database value as a character stream. (Java 1.2)

```
Clob getClob(int columnIndex)
Clob getClob(String columnName)
```
Returns a Clob locator, not the CLOB value. Use the Clob's getCharacterStream( ) method to retrieve the CLOB value using a Reader. (Java 1.2)

```
int getConcurrency( )
```
Returns this result set's concurrency mode, which will be one of the following constants (Java 1.2):

```
CONCUR_READ_ONLY
CONCUR_UPDATABLE
```

```
String getCursorName( )
```
Returns the name of the SQL cursor.

```
Date getDate(int columnIndex)
Date getDate(String columnName)
```
Returns a value as a java.sql.Date.

```
Date getDate(int columnIndex, Calendar calendar)
Date getDate(String columnName, Calendar calendar)
```
Returns a value as a java.sql.Date using the specified Calendar. (Java 1.2)

```
double getDouble(int columnIndex)
double getDouble(String columnName)
```
Returns a value as a double.

```
int getFetchDirection( )
```
Returns this result set's fetch direction as one of the following constants (Java 1.2):

```
FETCH_FORWARD
FETCH_REVERSE
FETCH_UNKNOWN
```

```
int getFetchSize( )
```
Returns the fetch size in rows. (Java 1.2)

```
float getFloat(int columnIndex)
float getFloat(String columnName)
```
Returns a value as a float.

```
int getInt(int columnIndex)
int getInt(String columnName)
```
Returns a value as an int.

```
long getLong(int columnIndex)
long getLong(String columnName)
```
Returns a value as a long.

```
ResultSetMetaData getMetaData( )
```
Returns a result set metadata object that in turn describes the result set.

```
Object getObject(int columnIndex)
Object getObject(String columnName)
```
Returns a database user-defined type (UDT) as a Java class using the current type map, or as a database-specific type using the driver's default mapping.

```
Object getObject(int columnIndex, Map map)
Object getObject(String columnName, Map map)
```
Returns a database UDT as a Java class using the type map specified, or returns a database-specific type using the driver's default mapping. (Java 1.2)

```
Ref getRef(int columnIndex)
Ref getRef(String columnName)
```
Returns a value as a Ref. (Java 1.2)

```
int getRow( )
```
Returns the current row number. (Java 1.2)

```
short getShort(int columnIndex)
short getShort(String columnName)
```
Returns a value as a short.

```
Statement getStatement( )
```
Returns this result set's Statement. (Java 1.2)

```
String getString(int columnIndex)
String getString(String columnName)
```
Returns a value as a String.

```
Time getTime(int columnIndex)
Time getTime(String columnName)
```
Returns a value as a Time.

```
Time getTime(int columnIndex, Calendar calendar)
Time getTime(String columnName, Calendar calendar)
```
   Returns a value as a Time using the specified Calendar. (Java 1.2)

```
Timestamp getTimestamp(int columnIndex)
Timestamp getTimestamp(String columnName)
```
   Returns a value as a Timestamp.

```
Timestamp getTimestamp(int columnIndex, Calendar calendar)
Timestamp getTimestamp(String columnName, Calendar calendar)
```
   Returns a value as a Timestamp using the specified Calendar.
   (Java 1.2)

```
int getType( )
```
   Returns this result set's type, which will match one of the
   following constants (Java 1.2):

```
        TYPE_FORWARD_ONLY
        TYPE_SCROLL_INSENSITIVE
        TYPE_SCROLL_SENSITIVE
```

```
URL getURL(int columnIndex)
URL getURL(String columnName)
```
   Returns a value as a java.net.URL. (Java 1.4)

```
SQLWarning getWarnings( )
```
   Returns the first SQL warning.

```
void insertRow( )
```
   Executes the "insert row" SQL statement, and then adds the
   row to the result set. (Java 1.2)

```
boolean isAfterLast( )
```
   Returns true if the cursor is after the last row. (Java 1.2)

```
boolean isBeforeFirst( )
```
   Returns true if the cursor is before the first row. (Java 1.2)

```
boolean isFirst( )
```
   Returns true if the cursor is on the first row. (Java 1.2)

```
boolean isLast( )
```
   Returns true if the cursor is on the last row. (Java 1.2)

```
boolean last( )
```
   Moves the cursor to the last row. (Java 1.2)

```
void moveToCurrentRow( )
```
   Moves the cursor to the row it was on before a call to
   moveToInsertRow( ). (Java 1.2)

```
void moveToInsertRow( )
```
Moves the cursor to the "insert row," a scratch pad row used to formulate a new row. (Java 1.2)

```
boolean next( )
```
Moves the cursor to the next row.

```
boolean previous( )
```
Moves the cursor to the previous row. (Java 1.2)

```
void refreshRow( )
```
Refreshes the current row with its current values in the database. (Java 1.2)

```
boolean relative(int rows)
```
Returns true if the cursor is successfully moved the relative number of rows forward for a positive value or backward for negative value. (Java 1.2)

```
boolean rowDeleted( )
```
Returns true if the current row has been deleted in the database. (Java 1.2)

```
boolean rowInserted( )
```
Returns true if the current row has been inserted into the database. (Java 1.2)

```
boolean rowUpdated( )
```
Returns true if the current row has been updated to the database. (Java 1.2)

```
void setFetchDirection(int direction)
```
Sets this result set's fetch direction. Use one of the following constants (Java 1.2):

```
FETCH_FORWARD
FETCH_REVERSE
FETCH_UNKNOWN
```

```
void setFetchSize(int rows)
```
Sets this result set's fetch size in rows. (Java 1.2)

NOTE

The following mutators or updateXXX( ) methods that have a columnIndex or columnName parameter all update a result set's column value for the specified column index (starting from 1, incrementing left to right), or column name, with the specified value.

```
void updateArray(int columnIndex, Array x)
void updateArray(String columnName, Array x)
```
   Updates a column value using the specified Array. (Java 1.4)

```
void updateAsciiStream(int columnIndex, InputStream x,
  int length)
void updateAsciiStream(String columnName, InputStream x,
  int length)
```
   Updates a column value using the specified ASCII stream and
   length. (Java 1.2)

```
void updateBigDecimal(int columnIndex, BigDecimal x)
void updateBigDecimal(String columnName, BigDecimal x)
```
   Updates a value using the specified java.math.BigDecimal.
   (Java 1.2)

```
void updateBinaryStream(int columnIndex, InputStream x,
  int length)
void updateBinaryStream(String columnName, InputStream x,
  int length)
```
   Updates a column value using the specified binary stream and
   length. (Java 1.2)

```
void updateBlob(int columnIndex, Blob x)
void updateBlob(String columnName, Blob x)
```
   Updates a column value using the specified Blob locator. Use
   Blob's setBinaryStream( ) method to update the BLOB value
   in the database. (Java 1.4)

```
void updateBoolean(int columnIndex, boolean x)
void updateBoolean(String columnName, boolean x)
```
   Updates a value using the specified boolean. (Java 1.2)

```
void updateByte(int columnIndex, byte x)
void updateByte(String columnName, byte x)
```
   Updates a value using the specified byte. (Java 1.2)

```
void updateBytes(int columnIndex, byte[ ] x)
void updateBytes(String columnName, byte[ ] x)
```
   Updates a value using the specified byte array. (Java 1.2)

```
void updateCharacterStream(int columnIndex, Reader x,
  int length)
void updateCharacterStream(String columnName, Reader x,
  int length)
```
   Updates a column value using the specified character stream
   and length. (Java 1.2)

```
void updateClob(int columnIndex, Clob x)
void updateClob(String columnName, Clob x)
```
Updates a column value using the specified Clob locator. Use Clob's setCharacterStream( ) method to update the CLOB value in the database. (Java 1.4)

```
void updateDate(int columnIndex, Date x)
void updateDate(String columnName, Date x)
```
Updates a value using the specified java.sql.Date. (Java 1.2)

```
void updateDouble(int columnIndex, double x)
void updateDouble(String columnName, double x)
```
Updates a value using the specified double. (Java 1.2)

```
void updateFloat(int columnIndex, float x)
void updateFloat(String columnName, float x)
```
Updates a value using the specified float. (Java 1.2)

```
void updateInt(int columnIndex, int x)
void updateInt(String columnName, int x)
```
Updates a value using the specified int. (Java 1.2)

```
void updateLong(int columnIndex, long x)
void updateLong(String columnName, long x)
```
Updates a value using the specified long. (Java 1.2)

```
void updateNull(int columnIndex)
void updateNull(String columnName)
```
Sets the specified column to NULL values. (Java 1.2)

```
void updateObject(int columnIndex, Object x)
void updateObject(String columnName, Object x)
```
Updates a value using the specified Object. (Java 1.2)

```
void updateObject(int columnIndex, Object x, int scale)
void updateObject(String columnName, Object x, int scale)
```
Updates a value using the specified Object and scale (for numeric data types). (Java 1.2)

```
void updateRef(int columnIndex, Ref x)
void updateRef(String columnName, Ref x)
```
Updates a column value using the specified Ref. (Java 1.4)

```
void updateRow( )
```
Updates the database by generating and executing an appropriate SQL statement. (Java 1.2)

```
void updateShort(int columnIndex, short x)
void updateShort(String columnName, short x)
```
Updates a value using the specified short. (Java 1.2)

```
void updateString(int columnIndex, String x)
void updateString(String columnName, String x)
```
Updates a value using the specified String. (Java 1.2)

```
void updateTime(int columnIndex, Time x)
void updateTime(String columnName, Time x)
```
Updates a value using the specified Time. (Java 1.2)

```
void updateTimestamp(int columnIndex, Timestamp x)
void updateTimestamp(String columnName, Timestamp x)
```
Updates a value using the specified Timestamp. (Java 1.2)

```
boolean wasNull( )
```
Returns true if the last column read contained an SQL NULL value.

ResultSetMetaData

Interface name: java.sql.ResultSetMetaData

ResultSetMetaData is used to programmatically determine the number of columns, their data types, and other attributes of a result set. All of its methods can throw an SQLException.

Fields

```
static int columnNoNulls
```
The column does not allow NULL values

```
static int columnNullable
```
The column allows NULL values

```
static int columnNullableUnknown
```
The nullability of a column's values is unknown

Methods

```
String getCatalogName(int columnIndex)
```
Returns a column's table's catalog name.

```
String getColumnClassName(int columnIndex)
```
Returns the fully-qualified Java class name that will be returned by ResultSet.getObject( ) if called for the specified column. (Java 1.2)

```
int getColumnCount( )
```
Returns the number of columns.

int getColumnDisplaySize(int columnIndex)
    Returns a column's maximum width in characters.

String getColumnLabel(int columnIndex)
    Returns a column's suggested label.

String getColumnName(int columnIndex)
    Returns a column's name.

int getColumnType(int columnIndex)
    Returns a column's type from java.sql.Types.

String getColumnTypeName(int columnIndex)
    Returns a column's database-specific type name.

int getPrecision(int columnIndex)
    Returns the number of decimal digits for a column.

int getScale(int columnIndex)
    Returns the number of digits to the right of the decimal point
    for a column.

String getSchemaName(int columnIndex)
    Returns a column's table's schema.

String getTableName(int columnIndex)
    Return a column's table name.

boolean isAutoIncrement(int columnIndex)
    Returns true if a column's numeric value is automatically
    assigned an incrementing number.

boolean isCaseSensitive(int columnIndex)
    Returns true if a column is case-sensitive.

boolean isCurrency(int columnIndex)
    Returns true if a column is a currency value.

boolean isDefinitelyWritable(int columnIndex)
    Returns true if a column is definitely writable.

int isNullable(int columnIndex)
    Returns the nullability of a column, which will be one of the
    following constants:

        columnNoNulls
        columnNullable
        columnNullableUnknown

boolean isReadOnly(int columnIndex)
    Returns true if a column is not writable.

```
boolean isSearchable(int columnIndex)
```
    Returns true if a column can be used in a WHERE clause.

```
boolean isSigned(int columnIndex)
```
    Returns true if numeric values in the column are signed.

```
boolean isWritable(int columnIndex)
```
    Returns true if a column is possibly writable.

RowSet
Java 1.4, JDBC 2.0 OP

Interface name: javax.sql.RowSet	Extends java.sql.ResultSet

RowSet extends the capabilities of ResultSet to add support to the JDBC API for the JavaBeans component model. This means that a RowSet can be used as a component in a visual Bean GUI development environment. RowSets can be used on or offline. Most of RowSet's methods can throw an SQLException.

Fields inherited from java.sql.ResultSet

```
static int CONCUR_READ_ONLY
static int CONCUR_UPDATABLE
static int FETCH_FORWARD
static int FETCH_REVERSE
static int FETCH_UNKNOWN
static int TYPE_FORWARD_ONLY
static int TYPE_SCROLL_INSENSITIVE
static int TYPE_SCROLL_SENSITIVE
```

Methods

```
void addRowSetListener(RowSetListener listener)
```
    Adds a rowset listener.

```
void clearParameters()
```
    Clears the command (SQL statement) parameter values, which are otherwise available for repeated use once they are set.

```
void execute()
```
    Executes the rowset's command (SQL statement) in order to fill the rowset with data.

```
String getCommand()
```
    Returns the rowset's command (SQL statement).

```
String getDataSourceName()
```
    Returns the JDBC data source's JNDI name.

`boolean getEscapeProcessing( )`

    Returns `true` if JDBC escape sequence support is enabled (the default).

`int getMaxFieldSize( )`

    Returns the maximum field size in bytes for BINARY, VARBINARY, LONGVARBINARY, CHAR, VARCHAR, and LONGVARCHAR columns.

`int getMaxRows( )`

    Returns the maximum number of rows that a rowset can contain.

`String getPassword( )`

    Returns the password used to establish the database connection.

`int getQueryTimeout( )`

    Returns the maximum amount of time the driver will wait for an SQL statement to execute, in seconds.

`int getTransactionIsolation( )`

    Returns the transaction isolation level as one of the following `Connection` constants:

```
TRANSACTION_NONE
TRANSACTION_READ_COMMITTED
TRANSACTION_READ_UNCOMMITTED
TRANSACTION_REPEATABLE_READ
TRANSACTION_SERIALIZABLE
```

`Map getTypeMap( )`

    Returns this rowset's type map.

`String getUrl( )`

    Returns the database URL used to establish this rowset's database connection.

`String getUsername( )`

    Returns the username used to establish the database connection.

`boolean isReadOnly( )`

    Returns `true` if this rowset can only be read.

`void removeRowSetListener(RowSetListener listener)`

    Removes a rowset listener.

NOTE

All of the following mutator or setXXX( ) methods set the specified parameter value for the specified parameter index (starting from 1, incrementing left to right) in the SQL statement.

---

void setArray(int i, Array x)
    Sets a value using the specified Array.

void setAsciiStream(int parameterIndex, InputStream x, int length)
    Sets a value using an ACSII input stream for length bytes.

void setBigDecimal(int parameterIndex, BigDecimal x)
    Sets a value using the specified java.math.BigDecimal.

void setBinaryStream(int parameterIndex, InputStream x, int length)
    Sets a value using a binary stream for length bytes.

void setBlob(int i, Blob x)
    Sets a BLOB locator, not the BLOB value.

void setBoolean(int parameterIndex, boolean x)
    Sets a value using the specified boolean.

void setByte(int parameterIndex, byte x)
    Sets a value using the specified byte.

void setBytes(int parameterIndex, byte[ ] x)
    Sets a value using the specified byte array.

void setCharacterStream(int parameterIndex, Reader reader, int length)
    Sets a value using a character stream for length characters.

void setClob(int i, Clob x)
    Sets a CLOB locator, not the CLOB value.

void setCommand(String sqlStatement)
    Sets the rowset's command (SQL query).

void setConcurrency(int concurrency)
    Sets the rowset's concurrency constant to one of the following:

        CONCUR_READ_ONLY
        CONCUR_UPDATABLE

---

void setDataSourceName(String name)
 Sets a rowset's data source name.

void setDate(int parameterIndex, Date x)
 Sets a value using the specified java.sql.Date.

void setDate(int parameterIndex, Date x, Calendar calendar)
 Sets a value using the specified java.sql.Date and Calendar.

void setDouble(int parameterIndex, double x)
 Sets a value using the specified double.

void setEscapeProcessing(boolean enable)
 Sets JDBC escape syntax support to on (if true) or off (if false).

void setFloat(int parameterIndex, float x)
 Sets a value using the specified float.

void setInt(int parameterIndex, int x)
 Sets a value using the specified int.

void setLong(int parameterIndex, long x)
 Sets a value using the specified long.

void setMaxFieldSize(int max)
 Sets the rowset's maximum field size for BINARY, VARBI-NARY, LONGVARBINARY, CHAR, VARCHAR, and LONGVARCHAR fields.

void setMaxRows(int max)
 Sets the maximum number of rows the rowset can contain.

void setNull(int parameterIndex, int javaSqlType)
 Sets a parameter to SQL NULL values.

void setNull(int parameterIndex, int javaSqlType,
 String typeName)
 Sets a parameter of a user-defined type (UDT) to SQL NULL values.

void setObject(int parameterIndex, Object x)
 Sets a value using the specified Object.

void setObject(int parameterIndex, Object x, int javaSqlType)
 Sets a value using the specified Object and java.sql.Types constant.

void setObject(int parameterIndex, Object x, int javaSqlType,
 int scale)
 Sets a value using the specified Object, java.sql.Types constant, and scale (for numeric data types).

void setPassword(String password)
>   Sets the password used to establish a database connection.

void setQueryTimeout(int seconds)
>   Sets the maximum amount of time the driver will wait for an SQL statement to execute, in seconds.

void setReadOnly(boolean value)
>   Sets the rowset to read-only.

void setRef(int i, Ref x)
>   Sets a value using the specified Ref.

void setShort(int parameterIndex, short x)
>   Sets a value using the specified short.

void setString(int parameterIndex, String x)
>   Sets a value using the specified String.

void setTime(int parameterIndex, Time x)
>   Sets a value using the specified Time.

void setTime(int parameterIndex, Time x, Calendar calendar)
>   Sets a value using the specified java.sql.Time and Calendar.

void setTimestamp(int parameterIndex, Timestamp x)
>   Sets a value using the specified Timestamp.

void setTimestamp(int parameterIndex, Timestamp x,
  Calendar calendar)
>   Sets a value using the specified java.sql.Timestamp and Calendar.

void setTransactionIsolation(int level)
>   Sets the transaction isolation; use one of the following Connection constants:
>
>   TRANSACTION_NONE
>   TRANSACTION_READ_COMMITTED
>   TRANSACTION_READ_UNCOMMITTED
>   TRANSACTION_REPEATABLE_READ
>   TRANSACTION_SERIALIZABLE

void setType(int type)
>   Sets the rowset's type; use one of the following constants:
>
>   TYPE_FORWARD_ONLY
>   TYPE_SCROLL_INSENSITIVE
>   TYPE_SCROLL_SENSITIVE

void setTypeMap(Map map)
>   Sets this rowset's default type map.

```
void setUrl(String url)
```
Sets the database URL used to establish a database connection.

```
void setUsername(String name)
```
Sets the username used to establish a database connection.

Methods inherited from java.sql.ResultSet

```
boolean absolute(int row)
void afterLast()
void beforeFirst()
void cancelRowUpdates()
void clearWarnings()
void close()
void deleteRow()
int findColumn(String columnName)
boolean first()
Array getArray(int columnIndex)
Array getArray(String columnName)
InputStream getAsciiStream(int columnIndex)
InputStream getAsciiStream(String columnName)
BigDecimal getBigDecimal(int columnIndex)
BigDecimal getBigDecimal(String columnName)
InputStream getBinaryStream(int columnIndex)
InputStream getBinaryStream(String columnName)
Blob getBlob(int columnIndex)
Blob getBlob(String columnName)
boolean getBoolean(int columnIndex)
boolean getBoolean(String columnName)
byte getByte(int columnIndex)
byte getByte(String columnName)
byte[ ] getBytes(int columnIndex)
byte[ ] getBytes(String columnName)
Returns the value as a byte array
Reader getCharacterStream(int columnIndex)
Reader getCharacterStream(String columnName)
Clob getClob(int columnIndex)
Clob getClob(String columnName)
int getConcurrency()
String getCursorName()
Date getDate(int columnIndex)
Date getDate(String columnName)
Date getDate(int columnIndex, Calendar calendar)
Date getDate(String columnName, Calendar calendar)
double getDouble(int columnIndex)
```

```
double getDouble(String columnName)
int getFetchDirection( )
int getFetchSize( )
float getFloat(int columnIndex)
float getFloat(String columnName)
int getInt(int columnIndex)
int getInt(String columnName)
long getLong(int columnIndex)
long getLong(String columnName)
ResultSetMetaData getMetaData( )
Object getObject(int columnIndex)
Object getObject(String columnName)
Object getObject(int columnIndex, Map map)
Object getObject(String columnName, Map map)
Ref getRef(int columnIndex)
Ref getRef(String columnName)
int getRow( )
short getShort(int columnIndex)
short getShort(String columnName)
Statement getStatement( )
String getString(int columnIndex)
String getString(String columnName)
Time getTime(int columnIndex)
Time getTime(String columnName)
Time getTime(int columnIndex, Calendar calendar)
Time getTime(String columnName, Calendar calendar)
Timestamp getTimestamp(int columnIndex)
Timestamp getTimestamp(String columnName)
Timestamp getTimestamp(int columnIndex, Calendar calendar)
Timestamp getTimestamp(String columnName, Calendar calendar)
int getType( )
URL getURL(int columnIndex)
URL getURL(String columnName)
SQLWarning getWarnings( )
void insertRow( )
boolean isAfterLast( )
boolean isBeforeFirst( )
boolean isFirst( )
boolean isLast( )
boolean last( )
void moveToCurrentRow( )
void moveToInsertRow( )
boolean next( )
boolean previous( )
void refreshRow( )
boolean relative(int rows)
```

```
boolean rowDeleted( )
boolean rowInserted( )
boolean rowUpdated( )
void setFetchDirection(int direction)
void setFetchSize(int rows)
void updateArray(int columnIndex, Array x)
void updateArray(String columnName, Array x)
void updateAsciiStream(int columnIndex, InputStream x,
   int length)
void updateAsciiStream(String columnName, InputStream x,
   int length)
void updateBigDecimal(int columnIndex, BigDecimal x)
void updateBigDecimal(String columnName, BigDecimal x)
void updateBinaryStream(int columnIndex, InputStream x,
   int length)
void updateBinaryStream(String columnName, InputStream x,
   int length)
void updateBlob(int columnIndex, Blob x)
void updateBlob(String columnName, Blob x)
void updateBoolean(int columnIndex, boolean x)
void updateBoolean(String columnName, boolean x)
void updateByte(int columnIndex, byte x)
void updateByte(String columnName, byte x)
void updateBytes(int columnIndex, byte[ ] x)
void updateBytes(String columnName, byte[ ] x)
void updateCharacterStream(int columnIndex, Reader x,
   int length)
void updateCharacterStream(String columnName, Reader x,
   int length)
void updateClob(int columnIndex, Clob x)
void updateClob(String columnName, Clob x)
void updateDate(int columnIndex, Date x)
void updateDate(String columnName, Date x)
void updateDouble(int columnIndex, double x)
void updateDouble(String columnName, double x)
void updateFloat(int columnIndex, float x)
void updateFloat(String columnName, float x)
void updateInt(int columnIndex, int x)
void updateInt(String columnName, int x)
void updateLong(int columnIndex, long x)
void updateLong(String columnName, long x)
void updateNull(int columnIndex)
void updateNull(String columnName)
void updateObject(int columnIndex, Object x)
void updateObject(String columnName, Object x)
void updateObject(int columnIndex, Object x, int scale)
```

```
void updateObject(String columnName, Object x, int scale)
void updateRef(int columnIndex, Ref x)
void updateRef(String columnName, Ref x)
void updateRow()
void updateShort(int columnIndex, short x)
void updateShort(String columnName, short x)
void updateString(int columnIndex, String x)
void updateString(String columnName, String x)
void updateTime(int columnIndex, Time x)
void updateTime(String columnName, Time x)
void updateTimestamp(int columnIndex, Timestamp x)
void updateTimestamp(String columnName, Timestamp x)
boolean wasNull()
```

RowSetEvent
Java 1.4, JDBC 2.0 OP

Class name: javax.sql.RowSetEvent | Extends java.util.EventObject

RowSetEvent is a row set–specific event.

Field inherited from class java.util.EventObject

source

Constructor

RowSetEvent(RowSet source)

Methods inherited from class java.util.EventObject

```
Object getSource()
String toString()
```

RowSetInternal
Java 1.4, JDBC 2.0 OP

Interface name: javax.sql.RowSetInternal

RowSetInternal is used to send or receive a rowset using a stream.
All of its methods can throw an SQLException.

Methods

Connection getConnection()
    Returns the rowset's connection.

ResultSet getOriginal()
    Returns a result set with the original values of the rowset.

ResultSet getOriginalRow( )
> Returns a result set with the original value of the current row.

Object[ ] getParams( )
> Returns the parameters for this rowset.

void setMetaData(RowSetMetaData md)
> Sets the rowset's metadata.

RowSetListener

Java 1.4, JDBC 2.0 OP

Interface name: javax.sql.RowSetListener   Extends java.util.EventListener

RowSetListener is implemented by any component that wishes to be notified when a change occurs in a rowset.

Methods

void cursorMoved(RowSetEvent event)
> Called by the rowset when its cursor moves.

void rowChanged(RowSetEvent event)
> Called by the rowset when a row is inserted, updated, or deleted.

void rowSetChanged(RowSetEvent event)
> Called by the rowset whenever it is changed.

RowSetMetaData

Java 1.4, JDBC 2.0 OP

Interface name: javax.sql.RowSetMetaData   Extends java.sql.ResultSetMetaData

RowSetMetaData is used to initialize a metadata object for a rowset. A RowSetReader may create a RowSetMetaData object and pass it to a rowset when new data is read. All of RowSetMetaData's methods can throw an SQLException.

Fields inherited from java.sql.ResultSetMetaData

columnNoNulls
columnNullable
columnNullableUnknown

Methods

void setAutoIncrement(int columnIndex, boolean property)
> If true, sets a column as one that is automatically numbered.

void setCaseSensitive(int columnIndex, boolean property)
> If true, sets a column as case-sensitive.

void setCatalogName(int columnIndex, String catalogName)
> Sets a column's table's catalog name.

void setColumnCount(int columnCount)
> Sets the number of columns in the rowset.

void setColumnDisplaySize(int columnIndex, int size)
> Sets a column's maximum width in characters.

void setColumnLabel(int columnIndex, String label)
> Sets a column's heading.

void setColumnName(int columnIndex, String columnName)
> Sets a column's name.

void setColumnType(int columnIndex, int javaSqlType)
> Sets a column's java.sql.Types type.

void setColumnTypeName(int columnIndex, String typeName)
> Sets a column's data source specific–type name.

void setCurrency(int columnIndex, boolean property)
> If true, sets the column as a currency value.

void setNullable(int columnIndex, int property)
> Sets the column's nullability; use one of the following constants:
>
>   columnNoNulls
>   columnNullable
>   columnNullableUnknown

void setPrecision(int columnIndex, int precision)
> Sets the number of decimal digits a column can have.

void setScale(int columnIndex, int scale)
> Sets the number of digits to right of the decimal point that a column can have.

void setSchemaName(int columnIndex, String schemaName)
> Sets a column's table's schema.

void setSearchable(int columnIndex, boolean property)
> If true, sets a column as one usable in a WHERE clause.

void setSigned(int columnIndex, boolean property)
> If true, sets a column as a signed number.

void setTableName(int columnIndex, String tableName)
> Sets a column's table name.

Methods inherited from java.sql.ResultSetMetaData

```
String getCatalogName(int columnIndex)
String getColumnClassName(int columnIndex)
int getColumnCount( )
int getColumnDisplaySize(int columnIndex)
String getColumnLabel(int columnIndex)
String getColumnName(int columnIndex)
int getColumnType(int columnIndex)
String getColumnTypeName(int columnIndex)
int getPrecision(int columnIndex)
int getScale(int columnIndex)
String getSchemaName(int columnIndex)
String getTableName(int columnIndex)
boolean isAutoIncrement(int columnIndex)
boolean isCaseSensitive(int columnIndex)
boolean isCurrency(int columnIndex)
boolean isDefinitelyWritable(int columnIndex)
int isNullable(int columnIndex)
boolean isReadOnly(int columnIndex)
boolean isSearchable(int columnIndex)
boolean isSigned(int columnIndex)
boolean isWritable(int columnIndex)
```

RowSetReader

Java 1.4, JDBC 2.0 OP

Interface name: javax.sql.RowSetReader

RowSetReader is implemented by any object that wishes to produce data for a rowset.

Method

```
void readData(RowSetInternal caller)
```
Read the source data for a rowset.

RowSetWriter

Java 1.4, JDBC 2.0 OP

Interface name: javax.sql.RowSetWriter

RowSetWriter is implemented by any object that wishes to persist data from a rowset.

Method

```
boolean writeData(RowSetInternal caller) throws SQLException
```
Writes the rowset data to its original data source.

Savepoint   Java 1.4

Interface name: java.sql.Savepoint

Savepoint represents a savepoint within the current transaction that can be referenced from the Connection's rollback( ) method to partially roll back a transaction. All of Savepoint's methods can throw an SQLException.

Methods

int getSavepointId( )
>   Returns the generated ID for this savepoint.

String getSavepointName( )
>   Returns the name of this savepoint.

SQLData   Java 1.2

Interface name: java.sql.SQLData

SQLData is implemented by any Java class that will be mapped to an SQL user-defined type (UDT). All of its methods can throw an SQLException.

Methods

String getSQLTypeName( )
>   Returns the fully-qualified name of the SQL UDT that the implementing class will represent.

void readSQL(SQLInput stream, String typeName)
>   Reads the data from the database using the stream's readXXX( ) methods.

void writeSQL(SQLOutput stream)
>   Writes the data to the database using the steam's writeXXX( ) methods.

SQLException

Class name: java.sql.SQLException

Extends java.lang.Exception
Implements java.io.Serializable
Subclasses: java.sql.BatchUpdateException, java.io.SQLWarning

SQLException is an SQL operation–specific exception used to report a database or JDBC driver error.

Constructors

```
SQLException( )
SQLException(String reason)
SQLException(String reason, String SQLState)
SQLException(String reason, String SQLState, int vendorCode)
```

Methods

int getErrorCode( )
> Returns the vendor's exception code.

SQLException getNextException( )
> Returns the next exception chained to this one.

String getSQLState( )
> Returns the SQLState.

void setNextException(SQLException ex)
> Chains an SQLException to the end of the exception chain.

SQLInput

Java 1.2

Interface name: java.sql.SQLInput

SQLInput is an input stream used by JDBC drivers to set the data values of a user-defined type (UDT) to a class that implements the SQLData interface. All of SQLInput's methods can throw an SQLException.

Methods

NOTE

The following accessor or readXXX( ) methods all return the next Java data type value from the stream. They are used in SQLData's readSQL( ) method.

Array readArray( )
> Returns a value as an Array.

InputStream readAsciiStream( )
> Returns an ASCII input stream.

BigDecimal readBigDecimal( )
> Returns a value as a java.math.BigDecimal.

InputStream readBinaryStream( )
    Returns a binary input stream.

Blob readBlob( )
    Returns a Blob locator. Use Blob's getBinaryStream( ) method
    to retrieve the BLOB value.

boolean readBoolean( )
    Returns a value as a boolean.

byte readByte( )
    Returns a value as a byte.

byte[ ] readBytes( )
    Returns a value as a byte array.

Reader readCharacterStream( )
    Returns a character input stream.

Clob readClob( )
    Returns a Clob locator. Use Clob's getCharacterStream( )
    method to retrieve the CLOB value.

Date readDate( )
    Returns a value as a java.sql.Date.

double readDouble( )
    Returns a value as a double.

float readFloat( )
    Returns a value as a float.

int readInt( )
    Returns a value as an int.

long readLong( )
    Returns a value as a long.

Object readObject( )
    Returns a value as an Object.

Ref readRef( )
    Returns a value as a Ref.

short readShort( )
    Returns a value as a short.

String readString( )
    Returns a value as a String.

Time readTime( )
    Returns a value as a Time.

Timestamp readTimestamp( )
  Returns a value as a Timestamp.

URL readURL( )
  Returns a value as a java.net.URL. (Java 1.4)

boolean wasNull( )
  Returns true if the last value read was an SQL NULL value.

SQLOutput

Java 1.2

Interface name: java.sql.SQLOutput

SQLOutput is an output stream used by JDBC drivers to get the data values of a user-defined type (UDT) from a class that implements the SQLData interface. All of SQLOutput's methods can throw an SQLException. (Java 1.2)

Methods

> **NOTE**
>
> The following mutator or writeXXX( ) methods all write the Java data type value to the output stream. They are all used in SQLData's writeSQL( ) method.

void writeArray(Array x)
  Writes a value as an Array.

void writeAsciiStream(InputStream x)
  Writes an ASCII input stream.

void writeBigDecimal(BigDecimal x)
  Writes a value as a java.math.BigDecimal.

void writeBinaryStream(InputStream x)
  Writes a binary input stream.

void writeBlob(Blob x)
  Writes a Blob locator.

void writeBoolean(boolean x)
  Writes a value as a boolean.

void writeByte(byte x)
  Writes a value as a byte.

void writeBytes(byte[ ] x)
  Writes a value as a byte array.

    void writeCharacterStream(Reader x)
        Writes a character input stream.

    void writeClob(Clob x)
        Writes a Clob locator.

    void writeDate(Date x)
        Writes a value as a java.sql.Date.

    void writeDouble(double x)
        Writes a value as a double.

    void writeFloat(float x)
        Writes a value as a float.

    void writeInt(int x)
        Writes a value as an int.

    void writeLong(long x)
        Writes a value as a long.

    void writeObject(SQLData x)
        Writes a value as an SQLData.

    void writeRef(Ref x)
        Writes a value as a Ref.

    void writeShort(short x)
        Writes a value as a short.

    void writeString(String x)
        Writes a value as a String.

    void writeStruct(Struct x)
        Writes a value as a Struct.

    void writeTime(Time x)
        Writes a value as a Time.

    void writeTimestamp(Timestamp x)
        Writes a value as a Timestamp.

    void writeURL(URL x)
        Writes a value as a java.net.URL. (Java 1.4)

SQLPermission

Java 1.3

Class name: java.sql.SQLPermission

Extends java.security.BasicPermission
Implements java.security.Guard, java.io.Serializable

SQLPermission represents the permission checked by SecurityManager when an applet calls one of the following JDBC log writer methods:

```
DriverManager.setLogWriter()
javax.sql.DataSource.setLogWriter()
javax.sql.ConnectionPoolDataSource.setLogWriter()
javax.sql.XADataSource.setLogWriter()
```

Without an SQLPermission object, these methods throw a java.
lang.SecurityException. The only target name currently
supported is setLog.

Constructors

```
SQLPermission(String targetName)
SQLPermission(String targetName, String actions)
```

NOTE

This SQLPermission class inherits methods from java.
security.BasicPermission and java.security.Permission.

SQLWarning

Class name: java.sql.SQLWarning

Extends java.sql.SQLException
Implements java.io.Serializable
Subclasses: java.sql.DataTruncation

SQLWarning is an SQL operation–specific exception used to report
a database or JDBC driver warning that is silently chained to a
JDBC object.

Constructors

```
SQLWarning()
SQLWarning(String reason)
SQLWarning(String reason, String SQLstate)
SQLWarning(String reason, String SQLstate, int vendorCode)
```

Methods

SQLWarning getNextWarning()
   Returns the next warning chained to this one.

void setNextWarning(SQLWarning w)
   Chains an SQLWarning to the end of the exception chain.

Methods inherited from java.sql.SQLException

```
int getErrorCode( )
SQLException getNextException( )
String getSQLState( )
void setNextException(SQLException ex)
```

Statement

Interface name: java.sql.Statement   Subinterfaces: java.sql.CallableStatement,
                                                          java.sql.PreparedStatement

Statement is an object used to execute a dynamic SQL statement. All of its methods can throw an SQLException.

Fields

static int CLOSE_ALL_RESULTS
  All result sets that have previously been kept open should be closed when calling getMoreResults( ).

static int CLOSE_CURRENT_RESULT
  The current result set should be closed when calling getMoreResults( ).

static int EXECUTE_FAILED
  An error occurred while executing a batch statement.

static int KEEP_CURRENT_RESULT
  The current result set should not be closed when calling getMoreResults( ).

static int NO_GENERATED_KEYS
  Generated keys should not be made available for retrieval.

static int RETURN_GENERATED_KEYS
  Generated keys should be made available for retrieval.

static int SUCCESS_NO_INFO
  A batch statement executed successfully, but no update count is available.

Methods

void addBatch(String sql)
  Adds the passed SQL statement sql to the current batch. (Java 1.2)

void cancel( )
  Cancels the current SQL statement.

```
void clearBatch( )
```
Clears SQL statements from the current batch. (Java 1.2)

```
void clearWarnings( )
```
Clears any SQL warnings.

```
void close( )
```
Closes the Statement object, which, in turn, immediately releases any database and JDBC resources. Not all JDBC implementations automatically close a Statement, so it is advisable to do so manually, as soon as possible, to conserve JDBC and database resources.

```
boolean execute(String sql)
```
Executes any dynamic DDL or DML SQL statement. Returns true if a result set is available, otherwise false.

```
boolean execute(String sql, int autoGeneratedKeys)
```
Executes any dynamic DDL or DML SQL statement while signaling the driver that any autogenerated keys should be made available for retrieval. Returns true if a result set is available, otherwise false. (Java 1.4)

```
boolean execute(String sql, int[ ] columnIndexes)
boolean execute(String sql, String[ ] columnNames)
```
Executes any dynamic DDL or DML SQL statement while signaling the driver that the autogenerated keys for the specified columns should be made available for retrieval. Returns true if a result set is available, otherwise false. (Java 1.4)

```
int[ ] executeBatch( )
```
Submits the current batch of commands to the database. Returns an array of update counts if all commands execute successfully. (Java 1.3)

```
ResultSet executeQuery(String sql)
```
Executes an SQL SELECT statement. Returns a result set containing the results of the query, or an empty result set if no data is found.

```
int executeUpdate(String sql)
```
Executes an SQL INSERT, UPDATE, or DELETE statement. Returns a count of the number of rows affected by the SQL statement.

```
int executeUpdate(String sql, int autoGeneratedKeys)
```
Executes an SQL INSERT, UPDATE, or DELETE statement while signaling the driver that any autogenerated keys should

be made available for retrieval. Returns a count of the number of rows affected by the SQL statement. (Java 1.4)

int executeUpdate(String sql, int[ ] columnIndexes)
int executeUpdate(String sql, String[ ] columnNames)

Executes an SQL INSERT, UPDATE, or DELETE statement while signaling the driver that any autogenerated keys for the specified columns should be made available for retrieval. Returns a count of the number of rows affected by the SQL statement. (Java 1.4)

Connection getConnection( )

Returns the Connection used to create this statement. (Java 1.2)

int getFetchDirection( )

Returns the current fetch direction for result sets created by this statement. The fetch direction will be one of the following constants (Java 1.2):

```
ResultSet.FETCH_FORWARD
ResultSet.FETCH_REVERSE
ResultSet.FETCH_UNKNOWN
```

int getFetchSize( )

Returns the default fetch size in rows. (Java 1.2)

ResultSet getGeneratedKeys( )

Returns a result set that contains any autogenerated keys created as a result of executing this Statement. (Java 1.4)

int getMaxFieldSize( )

Returns the maximum size of any column value in bytes.

int getMaxRows( )

Returns the maximum number of rows a result set can retrieve.

boolean getMoreResults( )

Returns true if the executed SQL statement produced a result set, otherwise false.

boolean getMoreResults(int current)

Returns true if there is another result set available. The disposition of the current result set, if any, is controlled by one of the following constants (Java 1.4):

```
CLOSE_CURRENT_RESULT
KEEP_CURRENT_RESULT
CLOSE_ALL_RESULTS
```

int getQueryTimeout( )

> Returns the amount of time, in seconds, the driver will wait for an SQL statement to execute before it times out.

ResultSet getResultSet( )

> Returns the current result set if one is available, otherwise null.

int getResultSetConcurrency( )

> Returns the result set concurrency for result sets created by this statement. It is one of the following constants (Java 1.2):
>
>   ResultSet.CONCUR_READ_ONLY
>   ResultSet.CONCUR_UPDATABLE

int getResultSetHoldability( )

> Returns the result set holdability setting for result sets generated by this Statement. It is one of the following constants (Java 1.4):
>
>   ResultSet.HOLD_CURSORS_OVER_COMMIT
>   ResultSet.CLOSE_CURSORS_AT_COMMIT

int getResultSetType( )

> Returns the result set type, as one of the following constants, for result sets created by this statement (Java 1.2):
>
>   ResultSet.TYPE_FORWARD_ONLY
>   ResultSet.TYPE_SCROLL_INSENSITIVE
>   ResultSet.TYPE_SCROLL_SENSITIVE

int getUpdateCount( )

> Returns the number of rows affected by an INSERT, UPDATE, or DELETE statement, 0 for a DDL statement, or -1 if a result set is available.

SQLWarning getWarnings( )

> Returns the first SQL warning reported for this statement.

void setCursorName(String name)

> Assigns the SQL cursor name to be used by this statement.

void setEscapeProcessing(boolean enable)

> Controls JDBC escape syntax processing. true turns on escape syntax processing, while false turns it off.

void setFetchDirection(int direction)

> Sets the default fetch direction for any subsequent result sets created by this statement. It is one of the following constants (Java 1.2):
>
>   ResultSet.FETCH_FORWARD
>   ResultSet.FETCH_REVERSE
>   ResultSet.FETCH_UNKNOWN

void setFetchSize(int rows)

    Sets the number of rows to fetch from the database as more rows are needed by any result sets created from the statement. (Java 1.2)

void setMaxFieldSize(int max)

    Sets the maximum size of any column value in bytes.

void setMaxRows(int max)

    Sets the maximum number of rows a ResultSet can retrieve.

void setQueryTimeout(int seconds)

    Sets the amount of time, in seconds, the driver will wait for an SQL statement to execute before it times out.

Struct   Java 1.2

Interface name: java.sql.Struct

Struct is the default mapping for an SQL user-defined type (UDT). A Struct contains a value for each attribute of the SQL UDT it represents. All of its methods can throw an SQLException.

Methods

Object[ ] getAttributes( )

    Returns an Object array that contains the data values of the SQL UDT in the same order as the attributes are defined in the UDT.

Object[ ] getAttributes(Map map)

    Returns an Object array that contains the data values of the SQL UDT in the same order as the attributes are defined in the UDT, using the specified type map.

String getSQLTypeName( )

    Returns the SQL UDT name.

Time

Class name: java.sql.Time

Extends java.util.Date
Implements: java.lang.Cloneable,
java.lang.Comparable, java.io.Serializable

Time is a wrapper class that allows JDBC to identify a column value as an SQL TIME value.

Constructor

Time(long timeInMillis)

Methods

void setTime(long timeInMillis)
> Sets the time in milliseconds.

String toString( )
> Formats the time in the JDBC date escape format: hh:mm:ss.

static Time valueOf(String s)
> Parses a string in JDBC date escape format to a Time value.

Methods inherited from java.util.Date

boolean after(Date when)
boolean before(Date when)
Object clone( )
int compareTo(Date anotherDate)
int compareTo(Object o)
boolean equals(Object obj)
long getTime( )
int hashCode( )

Timestamp

Class name: java.sql.Timestamp	Extends java.util.Date Implements java.lang.Cloneable, java.lang.Comparable, java.io.Serializable

Timestamp is a wrapper class that allows JDBC to identify a column value as an SQL TIMESTAMP value.

Constructor

Timestamp(long time)

Methods

boolean after(Timestamp ts)
> Returns true if this timestamp is a later time than the specified timestamp.

boolean before(Timestamp ts)
> Returns true if this timestamp is an earlier time than the specified timestamp.

int compareTo(Object o)
    Compares this Timestamp object to the specified Object.

int compareTo(Timestamp ts)
    Compares this Timestamp object to the specified Timestamp.
    (Java 1.2)

boolean equals(Object o)
    Returns true if this timestamp is equal to the specified object.

boolean equals(Timestamp ts)
    Returns true if this timestamp is equal to the specified
    timestamp.

int getNanos( )
    Returns this timestamp's nanosecond value.

void setNanos(int n)
    Sets this timestamp's nanosecond value.

void setTime(long time)
    Sets this timestamp to represent a point in time that is time
    milliseconds after January 1, 1970 00:00:00 GMT.

String toString( )
    Formats the timestamp in JDBC date escape format: yyyy-mm-
    dd hh:mm:ss.fffffffff.

static Timestamp valueOf(String s)
    Parses a string in JDBC date escape format to a Timestamp
    value.

Methods inherited from java.util.Date

```
boolean after(Date when)
boolean before(Date when)
Object clone( )
int compareTo(Date anotherDate)
long getTime( )
int hashCode( )
```

Throwable

Class name: java.lang.Throwable
Extends java.lang.Object
Implements java.io.Serializable
Subclasses: java.lang.Error, java.lang.Exception

Throwable is the superclass of all Java error and exception classes.

Constructors

```
Throwable( )
Throwable(String message)
```

Methods

`Throwable fillInStackTrace( )`
> Adds the current execution stack trace for the current thread to this Throwable.

`String getLocalizedMessage( )`
> Returns a locale-specific error message if overridden for this subclass.

`String getMessage( )`
> Returns an error message for this subclass.

`void printStackTrace( )`
> Prints this Throwable's stack trace and its back trace to the standard error.

`void printStackTrace(PrintStream s)`
> Prints this Throwable's stack trace and its back trace to the specified stream.

`void printStackTrace(PrintWriter s)`
> Prints this Throwable's stack trace and its back trace to the specified writer.

`String toString( )`
> Returns a description of this Throwable.

Types

Class name: java.sql.Types   Extends java.lang.Object

Types is a class that defines JDBC constants (XOPEN constant values) for SQL data types.

Fields

```
static int ARRAY (Java 1.2)
static int BIGINT
static int BINARY
static int BIT
static int BLOB (Java 1.2)
static int BOOLEAN (Java 1.4)
static int CHAR
```

```
static int CLOB (Java 1.2)
static int DATALINK (Java 1.4)
static int DATE
static int DECIMAL
static int DISTINCT (Java 1.2)
static int DOUBLE
static int FLOAT
static int INTEGER
static int JAVA_OBJECT (Java 1.2)
static int LONGVARBINARY
static int LONGVARCHAR
static int NULL
static int NUMERIC
static int OTHER
static int REAL
static int REF (Java 1.2)
static int SMALLINT
static int STRUCT (Java 1.2)
static int TIME
static int TIMESTAMP
static int TINYINT
static int VARBINARY
static int VARCHAR
```

XAConnection

Java 1.4, JDBC 2.0 OP

Interface name: javax.sql.XAConnection   Extends javax.sql.PooledConnection

XAConnection extends a PooledConnection to provide support for
distributed transactions.

Method

```
javax.transaction.xa.XAResource getXAResource( )
  throws SQLException
    Returns an XA resource.
```

Methods inherited from javax.sql.PooledConnection

```
void addConnectionEventListener(
    ConnectionEventListener listener)
void close( )
Connection getConnection( )
void removeConnectionEventListener(
    ConnectionEventListener listener)
```

XADataSource

Interface name: javax.sql.XADataSource

XADataSource is a factory for XAConnections. An XADataSource is typically retrieved via JNDI. All of its methods can throw an SQLException.

Methods

int getLoginTimeout( )

> Returns the maximum time that this data source can wait for a database connection, in seconds.

PrintWriter getLogWriter( )

> Returns the log writer for this data source.

XAConnection getXAConnection( )

> Returns an XA connection to the database.

XAConnection getXAConnection(String user, String password)

> Returns an XA connection to the database using the specified user and password to establish the database connection.

void setLoginTimeout(int seconds)

> Sets the maximum time that this data source will wait for a connection, in seconds.

void setLogWriter(PrintWriter out)

> Sets the log writer for this data source.

Other Titles Available from O'Reilly

Java

Java Performance Tuning, 2nd Edition

By Jack Shirazi
2nd Edition January 2003
600 pages, ISBN 0-596-00015-4

Significantly revised and expanded, this second edition not only covers Java 1.4, but adds new coverage of JDBC, NIO, Servlets, EJB and JavaServer Pages. The book remains a valuable resource for teaching developers how to create a tuning strategy, how to use profiling tools to understand a program's behavior, and how to avoid performance penalties from inefficient code, making them more efficient and effective. The result is code that's robust, maintainable and fast!

Java Network Programming, 2nd Edition

By Elliotte Rusty Harold
2nd Edition August 2000
760 pages, ISBN 1-56592-870-9

Java Network Programming, 2nd Edition, is a complete introduction to developing network programs (both applets and applications) using Java, covering everything from networking fundamentals to remote method invocation (RMI). It includes chapters on TCP and UDP sockets, multicasting protocol and content handlers, and servlets. This second edition also includes coverage of Java 1.1, 1.2 and 1.3.

Database Programming with JDBC and Java, 2nd Edition

By George Reese
2nd Edition August 2000
352 pages, ISBN 1-56592-616-1

This book describes the standard Java interfaces that make portable object-oriented access to relational databases possible, and offers a robust model for writing applications that are easy to maintain. The second edition has been completely updated for JDBC 2.0, and includes reference listings for JDBC and the most important RMI classes. The book begins with a quick overview of SQL for developers who may be asked to handle a database for the first time, and goes on to explain how to issue database queries and updates through SQL and JDBC.

Java Security, 2nd Edition

By Scott Oaks
2nd Edition May 2001
618 pages, ISBN 0-596-00157-6

The second edition focuses on the platform features of Java that provide security—the class loader, bytecode verifier, and security manager—and recent additions to Java that enhance this security model: digital signatures, security providers, and the access controller. The book covers in depth the security model of Java 2, version 1.3, including the two new security APIs: JAAS and JSSE.

O'REILLY®

To order: 800-998-9938 • *order@oreilly.com* • *www.oreilly.com*
Online editions of most O'Reilly titles are available by subscription at *safari.oreilly.com*
Also available at most retail and online bookstores.

Java Swing, 2nd Edition

By Marc Loy, Robert Eckstein, David Wood, James Elliott & Brian Cole
2nd Edition November 2002
1296 pages, ISBN 0-596-00408-7

This second edition of *Java Swing* thoroughly covers all the features available in Java 2 SDK 1.3 and 1.4. More than simply a reference, this new edition takes a practical approach. It is a book by developers for developers, with hundreds of useful examples, from beginning level to advanced, covering every component available in Swing. Whether you're a seasoned Java developer or just trying to find out what Java can do, you'll find *Java Swing*, 2nd edition an indispensable guide.

Java Programming with Oracle JDBC

By Donald K. Bales
1st Edition December 2001
496 pages, ISBN 0-596-00088-X

Here is the professional's guide to leveraging Java's JDBC in an Oracle environment. Readers learn the all-important mysteries of establishing database corrections; issuing SQL queries and getting results back; and advanced topics such as streaming large objects, calling PL/SQL procedures, and working with Oracle9*i*'s object-oriented features. Also covered: transactions, concurrency management and performance. This is an essential tool for all Java Oracle developers who need to work with both technologies.

Java Cookbook

By Ian Darwin
1st Edition June 2001
882 pages, ISBN 0-59600-170-3

This book offers Java developers short, focused pieces of code that are easy to incorporate into other programs. The idea is to focus on things that are useful, tricky, or both. The book's code segments cover all of the dominant APIs and many specialized APIs and should serve as a great "jumping-off place" for Java developers who want to get started in areas outside their specialization.

Java Enterprise Best Practices

By The O'Reilly Java Authors, edited by Robert Eckstein
1st Edition December 2002
304 pages, ISBN 0-596-00384-6

This book is for intermediate and advanced Java developers, the ones who have been around the block enough times to understand just how complex—and unruly—an enterprise system can get. Each chapter in this collection contains several rules that provide insight into the "best practices" for creating and maintaining projects using the Java Enterprise APIs. Written by the world's leading Java experts, this book covers JDBC, RMI/CORBA, Servlets, JavaServer Pages and custom tag libraries, XML, Internationalization, JavaMail, Enterprise JavaBeans, and performance tuning.

Java RMI

By William Grosso
1st Edition November 2001
576 pages, ISBN 1-56592-452-5

Enterprise Java developers, especially those working with Enterprise JavaBeans, and Jini, need to understand RMI technology in order to write today's complex, distributed applications. O'Reilly's *Java RMI* thoroughly explores and explains this powerful but often overlooked technology. Included is a wealth of real-world examples that developers can implement and customize.

Learning Java, 2nd Edition

By Pat Niemeyer &
Jonathan Knudsen
2nd Edition June 2002
832 pages, ISBN 0-596-00285-8

This new edition of *Learning Java* comprehensively addresses important topics such as web applications, servlets, and XML. It provides full coverage of all Java 1.4 language features including assertions and exception chaining as well as new APIs such as regular expressions and NIO, the new I/O package. New Swing features and components are described along with updated coverage of the JavaBeans component architecture using the open source NetBeans IDE the latest information about Applets and the Java Plug-in for all major browsers.

Java Best Practices

By The O'Reilly Java Authors,
edited by Robert Eckstein
1st Edition January 2003 (est.)
304 (est.) pages, ISBN 0-596-00385-4

This book is for intermediate and advanced Java developers, the ones who have used the traditional Java APIs enough to know that some methods work much better than others. Each chapter contains several tips and tricks that offer valuable insight into using the Java APIs—essentially, "best practices" for creating and maintaining projects using Java SDK software. Written by some of the world's leading Java experts, this book covers networking, security, collections, NIO, Swing, 2D, Internationalization, Java Beans, and performance tuning.

Java Management Extensions

By J. StevenPerry
1st Edition June 2002
312 pages, ISBN 0-596-00245-9

Java Management Extensions is a practical, hands-on guide to using the JMX APIs. This one-of-a kind book is a complete treatment of the JMX architecture (both the instrumentation level and the agent level), and it's loaded with real-world examples for implementing Management Extensions. It also contains useful information at the higher level about JMX (the "big picture") to help technical managers and architects who are evaluating various application management approaches and are considering JMX.

Java Servlet Programming, 2nd Edition

By Jason Hunter
with William Crawford
2nd Edition April 2001
780 pages, ISBN 0-596-00040-5

The second edition of this popular book has been completely updated to add the new features of the Java Servlet API Version 2.2, and new chapters on servlet security and advanced communication. In addition to complete coverage of the 2.2 specification, we have included bonus material on the new 2.3 version of the specification.

Java & XML, 2nd Edition

By Brett McLaughlin
2nd Edition September 2001
528 pages, ISBN 0-596-000197-5

New chapters on Advanced SAX, Advanced DOM, SOAP, and data binding, as well as new examples throughout, bring the second edition of *Java & XML* thoroughly up to date. Except for a concise introduction to XML basics, the book focuses entirely on using XML from Java applications. It's a worthy companion for Java developers working with XML or involved in messaging, web services, or the new peer-to-peer movement.

JavaServer Pages, 2nd Edition

By Hans Bergsten
2nd Edition August 2002
712 pages, ISBN 0-596-00317-X

Filled with useful examples and the depth, clarity, and attention to detail that made the first edition so popular with web developers, *JavaServer Pages*, 2nd Edition is completely revised and updated to cover the substantial changes in the 1.2 version of the JSP specifications, and includes coverage of the new JSTL Tag libraries—an eagerly anticipated standard set of JSP elements for the tasks needed in most JSP applications, as well as thorough coverage of Custom Tag Libraries.

Enterprise JavaBeans, 3rd Edition

By Richard Monson-Haefel
3rd Edition September 2001
592 pages, ISBN 0-596-00226-2

Enterprise JavaBeans has been thoroughly updated for the new EJB Specification. Important changes in Version 2.0 include a completely new CMP (container-managed persistence) model that allows for much more complex business function modeling; local interfaces that will significantly improve performance of EJB applications; and the "message driven bean," an entirely new kind of Java bean based on asynchronous messaging and the Java Message Service.

Java and XSLT

By Eric M. Burke
1st Edition September 2001
528 pages, ISBN 0-596-00143-6

Learn how to use XSL transformations in Java programs ranging from stand-alone applications to servlets. *Java and XSLT* introduces XSLT and then shows you how to apply transformations in real-world situations, such as developing a discussion forum, transforming documents from one form to another, and generating content for wireless devices.

Java Message Service

By Richard Monson-Haefel &
David Chappell
1st Edition December 2000
238 pages, ISBN 0-596-00068-5

This book is a thorough introduction to Java Message Service (JMS) from Sun Microsystems. It shows how to build applications using the point-to-point and publish-and-subscribe models; use features like transactions and durable subscriptions to make applications reliable; and use messaging within Enterprise JavaBeans. It also introduces a new EJB type, the MessageDrivenBean, that is part of EJB 2.0, and discusses integration of messaging into J2EE.

Java and SOAP

By Robert Englander
1st Edition May 2002
276 pages, ISBN 0-596-00175-4

Java and SOAP provides Java developers with an in-depth look at SOAP (the Simple Object Access Protocol). Of course, it covers the basics: what SOAP is, why it's soared to a spot on the Buzzwords' Top Ten list, and what its features and capabilities are. And it shows you how to work with some of the more common Java APIs in the SOAP world: Apache SOAP and GLUE.

Ant: The Definitive Guide

By Eric M. Burke & Jesse E. Tilly
1st Edition May 2002
288 pages, ISBN 0-596-00184-3

Ant is the premier build-management tool for Java environments. Ant is part of Jakarta, the Apache Software Foundation's open source Java project repository. Ant is written entirely in Java, and is platform independent. Using XML, a Java developer describes the modules involved in a build, and the dependencies between those modules. Ant then does the rest, compiling components as necessary in order to build the application.

O'REILLY®

To order: *800-998-9938* • *order@oreilly.com* • *www.oreilly.com*
Online editions of most O'Reilly titles are available by subscription at *safari.oreilly.com*
Also available at most retail and online bookstores.

Java & XML Data Binding

By Brett McLaughlin
1st Edition May 2002
214 pages, ISBN 0-596-00278-5

This new title provides an in-depth technical look at XML Data Binding. The book offers complete documentation of all features in both the Sun Microsystems JAXB API and popular open source alternative implementations (Enhydra Zeus, Exolabs Castor and Quick). It also gets into significant detail about when data binding is appropriate to use, and provides numerous practical examples of using data binding in applications.

NetBeans: The Definitive Guide

By Tim Boudreau, Jesse Glick, Simeon Greene, Vaughn Spurlin & Jack Woehr
1st Edition October 2002
696 pages, ISBN 0-596-00280-7

O'Reilly's *NetBeans: The Definitive Guide* is the authoritative reference for understanding and using the NetBeans Integrated Development Environment for creating new software with Java. Through a detailed tutorial, the book explains the capabilities of the NetBeans IDE, and compares it with competing software such as Borland's JBuilder. Then the authors go further, covering ways to expand NetBeans' basic capabilities by writing new modules for adding languages, new kinds of file storage, and collaborative capabilities, etc.

Programming Jakarta Struts

By Chuck Cavaness
1st Edition November 2002
464 pages, ISBN 0-596-00328-5

O'Reilly's *Programming Jakarta Struts* was written by Chuck Cavaness after his internet company decided to adopt the framework, then spent months really figuring out how to use it to its fullest potential. Readers will benefit from the real-world, "this is how to do it" approach Cavaness takes to developing complex enterprise applications using Struts, and his focus on the 1.1 version of the Framework makes this the most up-to-date book available.

Java NIO

By Ron Hitchens
1st Edition August 2002
312 pages, ISBN 0-596-00288-2

Java NIO explores the new I/O capabilities of version 1.4 in detail and shows you how to put these features to work to greatly improve the efficiency of the Java code you write. This compact volume examines the typical challenges that Java programmers face with I/O and shows you how to take advantage of the capabilities of the new I/O features. You'll learn how to put these tools to work using examples of common, real-world I/O problems and see how the new features have a direct impact on responsiveness, scalability, and reliability.

O'REILLY®

To order: *800-998-9938* • *order@oreilly.com* • *www.oreilly.com*
Online editions of most O'Reilly titles are available by subscription at *safari.oreilly.com*
Also available at most retail and online bookstores.

Java In a Nutshell
Quick References

Java Enterprise in a Nutshell, 2nd Edition

By David Flanagan, Jim Farley &
William Crawford
2nd Edition April 2002
992 pages, ISBN 0-596-00152-5

Completely revised and updated to
cover the new 2.0 version of Sun
Microsystems Java Enterprise Edition software, *Java Enterprise in a
Nutshell* 2nd edition covers the RMI,
Java IDL, JDBC, JNDI, Java Servlet,
and Enterprise JavaBeans APIs, with
a fast-paced tutorial and compact
reference material on each technology.

Java Foundation Classes in a Nutshell

By David Flanagan
1st Edition September 1999
748 pages, ISBN 1-56592-488-6

Java Foundation Classes in a Nutshell
provides an in-depth overview of the
important pieces of the (JFC), such
as the Swing components and Java
2D. It also includes compact reference
material on all the GUI- and graph-
ics-related classes in the numerous
javax.swing and java.awt packages.
Covers Java 2.

J2ME in a Nutshell

By Kim Topley
1st Edition, March 2002
462 pages, ISBN 0-596-00253-X

O'Reilly's *J2ME in a Nutshell* is as
definitive a reference to the heart of
the J2ME platform as the classic *Java
in a Nutshell* is for the Standard Java
platform. Its solid introduction to
J2ME covers the essential APIs for
different types of devices and
deployments; the profiles (specifications of the minimum sets of APIs
useful for a set-top box, wireless
phone, PDA, or other device); and
the Java virtual machine functions
that support those APIs. The meat of
the book is its classic O'Reilly-style
quick reference to all the core Micro
Edition classes.

Java in a Nutshell, 4th Edition

By David Flanagan
4th Edition March 2002
992 pages, ISBN 0-596-00283-1

This bestselling quick reference contains an accelerated introduction to
the Java programming language and
its key APIs, so seasoned programmers
can start writing Java code right
away. The fourth edition of *Java in a
Nutshell* covers the new Java 1.4 beta
edition, which contains significant
changes from the 1.3 version.

O'REILLY®

To order: *800-998-9938* • *order@oreilly.com* • *www.oreilly.com*
Online editions of most O'Reilly titles are available by subscription at *safari.oreilly.com*
Also available at most retail and online bookstores.

Java Examples in a Nutshell, 2nd Edition

By David Flanagan
2nd Edition September 2000
584 pages, ISBN 0-596-00039-1

In *Java Examples in a Nutshell*, the author of Java in a Nutshell has created an entire book of example programs that not only serve as great learning tools, but can also be modified for individual use. The second edition of this best-selling book covers Java 1.3, and includes new chapters on JSP and servlets, XML, Swing, and Java 2D. This is the book for those who learn best "by example."

JXTA in a Nutshell

By Scott Oaks, Bernard Traversat &
Li Gong
1st Edition September 2002
416 pages, ISBN 0-596-00236-X

O'Reilly's pioneering reference is the first and last word on this powerful distributed computing technology. *JXTA in a Nutshell* delivers all the information you need to get started, including an overview of P2P distributed computing, an explanation of the JXTA Project's new platform, and ways that developers can become a part of the development effort. *JXTA in a Nutshell* introduces major concepts in a hands-on way by explaining them in context to the shell, and contains a complete reference to the JXTA application bindings. Also included is the full JXTA protocol specification. The book covers important topics such as security, and how the JXTA technology fits into the standard Java classes.